TELL ME I BELONG

TELL ME I BELONG

A Journey Across Faiths and Generations

DAVID WEILL

UNION SQUARE & CO.
NEW YORK

ISBN 978-1-4549-6183-3
ISBN 978-1-4549-6184-0 (e-book)

Library of Congress Control Number: 2025942837

Union Square & Co. books may be purchased in bulk for business, educational, or promotional use. For more information, please contact your local bookseller or the Hachette Book Group's Special Markets department at special.markets@hbgusa.com.

Printed in Canada

Printing 1, 2025

unionsquareandco.com

Cover design by Patrick Sullivan
Cover images by Shutterstock.com: 32 pixels (compass vector), Andrey_Kuzmin (brass compass), Artistdesign.13 (burst)
Interior design by Marie Mundaca
Interior images courtesy of David Weill, with the exception of the *Leopoldstadt* marquee and the Tel Aviv sign (Alamy)

For my mother, Kathleen Burton Weill, whose legacy I am proud to carry. I love you, mom.

Every man is a bridge, spanning the legacy he inherited
and the legacy he passes on.

—Terrence Real

The unexamined life is not worth living.

—Socrates

AUTHOR'S NOTE

PEOPLE TELL THEMSELVES STORIES ABOUT WHO THEY ARE. In the absence of solid information or undisputable truths, they fill in the blanks with whatever narrative serves them best.

We are a mother or a father, a husband or a wife, a sister or a brother. We are a person of color; we are White. We are conservatives or progressives. We live in a blue state or a red one. We are Jews or Gentiles, Hindu or Muslim.

Personal identification is on the rise, some say, but we have always trafficked in it. It's tribal—it's what humans do—going all the way back to the beginning of recorded history.

But what happens when what we know about ourselves, where we came from, what preceded us, our very foundation, is all a big blur, spoken in fragments, or worse, not spoken at all?

This is what happens: We live our lives rudderless, left wondering. We live with insecurity—and we search. Sometimes what we find is good, but sometimes what we find horrifies us. But it is ours, nonetheless.

Until recently, my story could only be punched out in fragmented bursts. I am the son of an agnostic Holocaust survivor and a Baptist mother from Selma, Alabama. As such, while growing up in New

Orleans, I fit neatly neither into the well-established Jewish community nor into the gentile, and genteel, aristocratic crowd. I had an identity problem that was manifested by insecurity, the feeling that I never quite belonged, masked for many years by the transplant doctor bravado I so carefully cultivated. The gratitude from my patients that I yearned for—and earned—provided sustaining nourishment that drove me forward.

And that strategy worked, until it didn't.

This book is about what I did when the trail defining my own identity went cold—and what I decided to do when that cold trail I had been living on for the first six decades of my life would no longer do. The search is why I wrote the pages you are about to read, the ones I have spent a lifetime contemplating, ruminating about, and agonizing over.

Although I am just now putting this story on the pages that follow, I have been writing it my entire life. My journey started early in life, from the time when as a young boy, my parents asked if I wanted a religious life (I said no), to the trips to the Black New Orleans churches where I would go with a woman who worked in our house and whom I considered my second mother, to the family trips to Miami Beach to visit my grandfather who had spent several weeks in a concentration camp before emigrating to the United States. My summer visits to Selma were spent reconciling the comments of my racist grandparents with my mother's clandestine trips with my two sisters and me to the Edmund Pettus Bridge, propelled by her hope that her kids would understand what she stood for: the side of justice.

That's how it was, a confusing background that made even the simple question unanswerable, whether posed on the schoolyard as a boy, or at a party, or on a date when I was older: "*What religion are you?*" My easiest answer to this question—a straightforward one for most—was laced with humor as a means to deflect from the larger issue: "*How much time do you have?"* The Big Question was, and to some extent still is, an anxiety-producing one—a mixture of shame, embarrassment, and resentment because of my complicated family history.

To someone who is not prone to feel fear, in fact was trained as a transplant doctor not to feel anything, these emotions haunted me my entire life, a gnawing part of my psyche that stood in stark distinction to the rest of my life, one that was filled with so much that was positive. This book is my way of saying, *Enough*—enough of the not knowing, enough of the not understanding who my family was and, therefore, who I am. In these pages, you will see, I will shine a light on the dark corners of my past, explaining an ancestry that up until now was left unexplained.

I have divided the book into four sections. The first explains how little I knew of my own family's heritage, their struggles, their attitudes toward religion—and how that lack of understanding shaped my early life. The second part chronicles my search to find out more about my family's circumstances, the twists and turns, and the experiences of those who came before me. The third part describes my inheritance—the part I knew about and the part I didn't. And in the last part, I will share how all of what I now know has determined where I have landed, my understanding of who I really am, my true identity.

I know I am not alone in this quest—there are many readers just like me, those who want to reconcile where they came from with who they are now. My hope is that my journey brings you comfort, solace in a world where we all could use some. It has for me.

David Weill
New Orleans

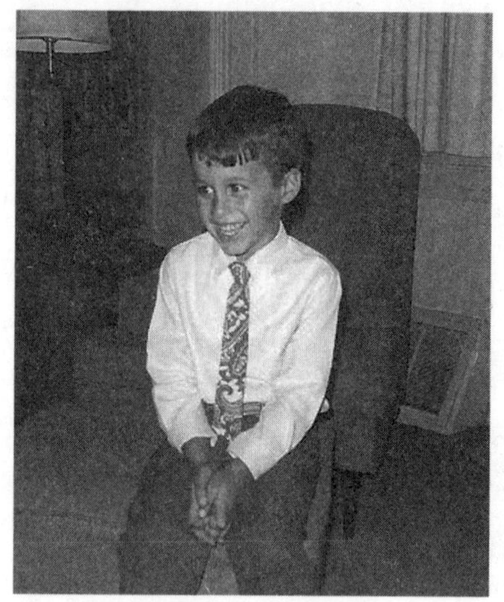

The author, 1969

PROLOGUE

New Orleans, 1972

I WAS SURE SOMEONE WAS LURKING OUTSIDE THE DRESSING room, a terrorist who wanted to kill me.

At eight years old, my imagination may have gotten the best of me—I say that now with the benefit of adult retrospection. But were my thoughts back then really that far-fetched?

My mother had taken me to a large department store in downtown New Orleans that day to buy clothes for the upcoming school year. I tried on a pair of pants that were too short and a turtleneck that was too tight around my neck, a scratchy vise that was ill-suited for the tropical climate of my hometown. But my thoughts were not on which clothes to buy. I was focused on what I heard that morning.

Like most of the world during those last days of summer in 1972, I was glued to the TV set, watching the Munich Olympic Games.

Always a spectacle of sorts, these Games were even more remarkable given that it was only the second time in history that Germany had hosted the Olympics. The first time was in 1936, a Nazi propaganda display, an eruption of nationalism that, in retrospect and in real time, was a dark, grotesque preview of things to come.

But the Munich Games started off differently. Mark Spitz, an American swimmer, had won seven gold medals, demolishing the competition in each of his events—and was Jewish, as my father pointed out as we watched him swim away from the field time and time again. With his record-setting athletic achievements and his good looks, he had won over the world. My father, a German emigrant to the United States in 1939, was watching with special interest as the country of his birth held the Olympics, a chance for Germany to show a different face to the world as host of "Die Heiteren Spiche," as the Germans had promoted the event: "The Cheerful Games." I think my father was curious to see if things had really changed. Along with the rest of the world, he was skeptical.

He had reason to be. The ABC broadcaster Jim McKay broke into the telecast early one morning and said that eleven Israeli Olympic athletes had been taken hostage by a pro-Palestinian terrorist group called Black September. I can remember how ominous the group's name sounded to my young ears. *Black September? Why was it Black?*

If their demands were not met, McKay said as I watched from a seat on the living room floor, my back against the couch where my father sat, the hostages would be killed, as well as one Jew per hour around the world, selected at random presumably, until more than two hundred Palestinian prisoners held in Israeli jails were released. Those were the stark facts that I heard coming from our TV set, one of my first introductions to the realities of the world. I felt my stomach drop. I was in danger—*we* were in danger, even though I was only vaguely aware of my father's Jewish heritage. Knowing that he might be Jewish—perhaps even *probably* was Jewish—was enough to frighten me, to shake my young world.

I looked up at my father, who sat still, expressionless, slowly drinking a glass of orange juice. He had seen this movie before.

By early the next morning, the Israeli athletes were dead. In a moment of television history that none of us would ever forget, we were fixated on the flickering images, similar to when Neil Armstrong landed on the moon, the United States Embassy in Saigon was evacuated by helicopter, and the Twin Towers fell. McKay said in a solemn voice, like an actor coming out of character, "Our greatest hopes and our worst fears are seldom realized." But on this September morning, no one really believed that, including me, who had been allowed to stay up until dawn to watch.

My worst fears would be realized, soon, or so I thought.

The next thing McKay said stuck with me: "They're all gone." That much I understood. I didn't have to imagine or anticipate the worst.

Sitting in the dressing room later that afternoon in New Orleans, thousands of miles away from Munich or Israel or anywhere else of geopolitical significance, I felt as though I was waiting my turn, not for the attendant to ask how I liked the clothes, how was the fit, but rather for the terrorists with guns, the ski-masked men with automatic weapons to burst through the curtains of my changing room at any second. I could be next, or so I was convinced.

Was I just a boy with an active imagination?

Or was it because I thought I was Jewish? *My father was Jewish, right, wasn't he? So wasn't I Jewish as well?*

* * *

But the more vexing question is, *why did I think that?* I was born to a father who practiced no religion, though he was ostensibly Jewish, and who often quoted Karl Marx, despite my father's fervent anti-communism sentiment, when Marx said that religion was the opium of the masses. But if a quasi-feeling of Jewishness didn't come from my father's ambiguous relationship with religion, where did it come from? My eight-year-old feeling of Jewishness couldn't have been based on my mother's religious background—she was from a Southern Baptist family who as a young girl went to church "any time they opened the door."

So what was on the mind of that scared little boy that day? It could have been inherited trauma—a concept that was not recognized in the early seventies—but eventually would be defined as "generational trauma that is unresolved trauma and shame inherited from one's parents through epigenetic inheritance." It is essentially "family trauma" because we inherit it from our parents, just as surely as we inherit things like eye color certainly, but also mannerisms that are not likely to be genetically determined but rather "epigenetic," or circumstantial inheritance. In other words, if you grow up in your parents' home, all of their traits are in play, not just the characteristics that are passed through their DNA. Your parents' experiences—the good and the bad—become your experiences, even if you never lived them. Even as an eight-year-old, I knew that there were a group of bad people (in this case, Nazis) who had tried to kill my father and members of his/my family. That experience had traumatized them—and, apparently, me.

And so, even in the safest of circumstances—a boy with his mother in the familiarity of his hometown, usually not a care in the world except what was for dinner and when was the next basketball game—there I sat: afraid, insecure, sure that "they" were coming for me. Because I was Jewish.

Which was odd. Because then, I didn't identify as such.

But how did I identify? Well, that, as it turns out, would be the central question that would chase, haunt, frustrate, embarrass, and quite generally gnaw at me from the time I sat in that department store dressing room until recently when, once and for all, I tried to figure it out, what my identity truly is and how I fit into this world.

But the search doesn't follow a straight line—like all searches, the path goes here and then there, each step along the way providing another building block for the person I would become.

As you shall see, some answers were forthcoming, some weren't. But in the search, I came closer to what I have wanted all along: understanding.

PART ONE

UNEASINESS

The son wishes to remember what the father wishes to forget.

—*Yiddish Proverb*

Menorah from the author's grandfather, Kurt Weill

CHAPTER ONE

DO YOU WANT RELIGION IN YOUR LIFE?

New Orleans, 1973

I WAS A NINE-YEAR-OLD BOY WHEN MY PARENTS SUMMONED me to meet with them, a rare occurrence that probably meant something significant was about to happen. I just didn't know then *how* significant.

Like most days, I was lying flat in bed with my basketball, practicing my shot over and over. My parents had asked my sisters and me to talk with them individually in the dining room according to age, oldest to youngest, a procedure set forth by my German father for whom order and process superseded all else. I was last and had been waiting for what felt like an eternity. My 8-track cassette player was playing the new Paul McCartney and Wings album *Band on the Run*, the volume turned down low so I would be able to hear when my parents called me.

What do they want to talk to us about?

My sister Leslie, who was twelve at the time, stood in my doorway. "Your turn," she said.

"Was it bad?" I asked. "Are we in trouble?" She shook her head no and gave me a punch in the arm, for good measure, before I ran upstairs, two steps at a time.

Our dining room was on the upper level, as was our kitchen and my parents' bedroom—a common setup in old Louisiana homes because of the very real possibility of floodwaters coming over the levees. The kids' bedrooms and bathroom were downstairs—it was okay if those rooms flooded, I supposed at the time.

When I reached the top of the stairs, I set my basketball down on the landing—my parents hated it when I brought the ball into the dining room—and stepped through the doorway.

Our dining room was formal, with creaking hardwood floors, antique furniture, and a long table in the center surrounded by eight upholstered chairs. Underneath the table was an Oriental rug that was more than a hundred years old. Overhead hung a chandelier from my grandfather's antique collection, a few cobwebs stretching between the candlesticks. On top of the cabinet that held my mother's fine china was a violin, one apparently owned by our relative, the composer Kurt Weill. We were not permitted to touch it, so I assumed Kurt Weill was someone important. Next to the violin was a silver menorah that no one in my family ever touched either, for different reasons, out of reach but always in view.

I always kept one eye on it. *I could reach out and touch it if I wanted to, couldn't I?*

That day, and most days, my father sat at the head of the table, my mother next to him on the side. When I came in, he gestured to a chair opposite my mother. I sat down.

"Your mother and I have been talking," he said, "and we want to know whether you want to keep going to synagogue regularly."

I was puzzled by the question, given that we had never gone to synagogue, either regularly or irregularly. As a matter of fact, I can't recall ever being there. "Is it important to you? Or are you just going to complain about it each Saturday?" my father asked, less like a question and more like a commentary on what he thought was most likely.

I don't remember complaining about going to services, because I don't remember ever going. But, as I look back on it now, it was sort of a silly question, or at the very least, rhetorical: What kid wouldn't complain about going to church or synagogue? My feet dangled above the floor—our dining room chairs were far too big for a child—as I considered what my father was saying. I wondered if he was asking a trick question, but then, unable to identify any ulterior motive, I became suddenly astonished that my parents were asking my opinion at all, especially about something this consequential.

Is this happening? Are my parents really making this religion thing my call?

My father stared at me, waiting for an answer.

I thought about it for a second. *Let's see: Waste precious weekend hours in a neck-scratching turtleneck and blazer, or be allowed to play basketball, watch football on TV, and hang out with my friends all day? Was this even a question?*

"No," I said slowly, trying to pretend that I was actually giving the question careful consideration. "I guess I'd rather not go. I think I'm okay without it." I sat there, trying to wear an expressionless mask—and I waited.

My parents looked at each other.

"Okay, that's it," my father finally said, waving his hand. "You can go."

I leapt out of my chair before he could ask more probing questions, before my parents could change their minds and set the family on a religious path of no return.

I don't know why my parents asked us to make the decision about whether we would be a religious family. Were their questions to us about what direction our spiritual life would take reflective of their own ambivalence about religion? Like a good courtroom lawyer, did my father know the answer to the question before he asked it, eliciting a response that would be supportive of his own skepticism about religion generally, and his own, specifically?

He died in 2013. I can't ask him these questions now, and didn't while he was alive, in keeping with our family's tendency to suppress our faith, whatever label each of us would eventually give it.

But why was religion an unspoken subject in our house in the same way other families might have things "we don't talk about"? What was the avoidance imperative?

So the path was set, my spiritual destiny uncertain, setting into motion a life of searching for an elusive sense of belonging to something, to anything that I could call my own.

CHAPTER TWO

MISS DEBORAH

New Orleans, 1975

The author and Deborah Badon, 2015

LIKE MANY UPPER-MIDDLE-CLASS HOUSEHOLDS IN THE SOUTH, and New Orleans in particular, our family had domestic help—a member of our household that wasn't family, technically at least, but really *was* family. In our house, that presence was Deborah Badon, a Black woman with an easy smile and a sharp wit, who believed in big hugs and stern discipline, handed out equally, alternating between one and the other without a moment's notice. She wasn't afraid to call out anyone who was doing the wrong thing, including my father, who wasn't accustomed to, or fond of, being challenged.

From the time I was born, nearly every day, the face I saw when I first awoke, at meals, and even in the evenings before I went to bed, was Deborah's. She drove to our house each morning, parked her car in front, and cheerfully took on the business of helping my mother with the cleaning, cooking, and care of my two older sisters and me. That's not to say that my mother sat around and did nothing, drinking mint juleps on the veranda or whatever the cliché of life in the South evokes. No, it wasn't like that at all. My mother provided a loving, warm home environment—and could always be counted on for age-appropriate book recommendations.

I felt as though I had two mother figures, two people to provide whatever I needed—and whenever I needed it. This was at least the way my treatment was described by my two older sisters, Judy and Leslie, who have often said I was the prince of the family, an opinion that I choose to attribute to the common sentiment that another sibling was always getting a better deal.

My mother and Deborah were partners, friends really, who performed the endless tasks required to keep afloat a household with young children and a work-obsessed father. Both of them took breaks during the day, my mother to dive into one of her books, Deborah to watch *Soul Train* or one of her "stories" on the black-and-white TV in our kitchen. Most days before I was old enough to go to school, or after school when I started to attend school, I sat on the couch with Deborah and watched Don Cornelius, the host of *Soul Train*, introduce the musical guests. I listened closely to the music and marveled at the young men and women dancing in the studio. Deborah gently swayed to the music while ironing my father's dress shirts, keeping one eye on her work and the other on the TV. To this day, the soul music of the sixties and seventies is my favorite, bringing me immediately back to the kitchen in my childhood home, to a time that I cherished. Occasionally, I would look over at my mother, sitting in her favorite chair, sipping her tea, smiling at me. I watched both of them, their every move, feeling lucky to have these two women in my life. Even now as I look back on those long afternoons spent in that room, I can't recall another time when I felt more loved or more protected.

My father was an academic physician of significant renown and, as a result of his position, traveled a great deal, lecturing all over the world and meeting colleagues in other research units that did similar work in the occupational lung disease realm. My mother reluctantly went with him, especially when my sisters and I were young, but she didn't share my father's interest, either for travel in general or for drinks and dinner with his professional connections in particular. She would rather, as she told me and him, have been at home, spending time with us, perhaps with a gin and tonic or two and a good book.

Miss Deborah would stay with us when my parents were away, sometimes leaving her own son at home with her husband and, at other times, bringing him over to spend the night with us. Her son, Michael, was about my age and we had the same interests: sports, climbing down to the edge of a waterway by our house, looking for, and usually finding, rodents of all kinds—rats, nutria, snakes, and the odd raccoon. This was South Louisiana, after all. We would take shots at them with a BB gun that I borrowed from a friend. A decade or so later, Michael was shot with a real gun while walking in his neighborhood in a case of mistaken identity but was fortunately not killed. Michael and I shared Deborah, but our start in life couldn't have been more different. His circumstances were not mine, and mine, not his.

But what was the most memorable of these times, when Deborah was in charge of us, were the visits on Sunday morning to her church. Deborah attended a Baptist church in one of the poorer sections of town, an area that was nearly all Black and one to which I wasn't afraid to travel. The stereotype that all Black neighborhoods were "dangerous" hadn't been developed within me.

I sat in the pews holding Deborah's hand, mine the only White face in a church full of Black parishioners. One of the first things I noticed was how well dressed everyone was. The men in suits, the women in long dresses and hats, despite the smothering heat of New Orleans summers. The children were similarly attired, looking as uncomfortable as I was. My dress shoes were too tight, and the long pants and dress shirts I wore would be ripped off as soon as I got home, replaced with T-shirts and shorts.

But it wasn't just the clothes that made this place special—it was the sense of community. Before the service started, parishioners greeted one another, smiling and laughing, asking each other about their children, their mothers. From all appearances, they weren't just asking to be polite but rather because they really wanted to know. "Your mama not feeling well," Deborah would say, "I'll bring her over a nice gumbo. That'll make her feel better." And she was right: Her gumbo did make people feel better.

The real magic though happened when the service started. The preacher at the pulpit would deliver his sermon with all his might, the congregation giving back steady affirmation. "Say it," "That's right," "Amen," "Preach it, my brother," the parishioners would say, at just the right time. And the singing, the joyous, rapturous singing. The congregation would clap their hands and stomp their feet, bringing a smile to my young face as my head quickly swiveled around, looking left and right, back and forth, to make sure I caught it all. The memory of this scene returns the smile to my face now, over five decades later.

Even then, I thought that if one couldn't feel the Lord in this house, then one couldn't feel God at all. Having never gone to a synagogue or another church, I thought, *this is religion*. It wasn't my religion, I knew that. The people didn't look like me, act like people I knew, my only connection to it was through an extraordinary woman who worked in our house. I was at least aware of that. But if I wasn't part of *that*, what was I part of? I wasn't sure if I was Baptist. I could have been. *Wasn't my mother?* But I sure knew that I wasn't a member of this church and I wasn't Black, especially obvious when I looked down at Deborah's Black hand in mine.

She would turn her hand over, palm face down and say, "This is the Black side," then turn it the other way, palm up, with her hand still in mine, and say, "And this is the White side, just like yours." I would stare at both of our hands, her hand with a Black and White side, and mine with only White sides. I looked up at her smiling face and nodded, thinking, *Was that all there was to this Black and White thing, a difference in one side of the hand from the other? Did I belong here in this church with Deborah or was I just a guest, affiliated through a parishioner to whom I was close?*

When the service would end and everyone started to file out into the midday heat, I would walk closely behind Deborah. Occasionally someone would stop her and ask, "Who is this cute little boy?" I grabbed a piece of Deborah, an arm, a leg, the bottom of her dress, a blushing White child in a sea of Black love. I always remember walking out of that church feeling better than when I walked in. *Was this religion? Had I found it deep inside my hometown, in the Black part of New Orleans?*

That was my first real encounter with religion: joyful, meaningful, connected, love. Unambiguous. Simple.

Religion wouldn't stay that way for me, not by a long shot. I would venture far from that modest church in inner-city New Orleans to a place of confusion, ambivalence—and even shame.

The author on the Isidore Newman basketball team, 1982

CHAPTER THREE

THE (FIRST) TIME I WAS CALLED A KIKE

New Orleans, 1979

EVEN IF I WASN'T SURE IF I WAS JEWISH, OTHER PEOPLE seemed to be.

As someone who did not have religion in my life, I found my own growing up: basketball. Yes, I know, it's not really a religion, but I treated it that way. Sure, I did other things: took family trips to the beach, rode my bike around New Orleans on hot summer afternoons when the entire town was mine for the taking, hung out by the pool with my friends.

But my first love affair? Basketball. That was the main/only thing. Ironically, my first basketball uniform when I was seven had a Star of David on the front. My parents registered me in a league at the New Orleans Jewish Community Center. We played games every Sunday morning and had practices during the week. I knew most of the kids who played in the league, Jews and Gentiles who may not have shared a religion but only a love of the game. We all called the league the JBA, or the Jewish Basketball Association, a play on the National Basketball Association, or NBA, a slightly mocking but good-natured label. As someone without religious affiliation, I wasn't offended.

As time went on, I played hoops with my friends day and night and would go off to basketball camps for weeks at a time in the summer to learn, practice, and compete against the best young players in the country. I set up my own private basketball clinic in the driveway of our house, dribbling around cones, alternating hands, going backwards and forwards and side to side with eyes open, then closed. I made an X-shaped target on the garage door with duct tape and tried to hit it with chest, bounce, and behind-the-back passes, using my left and right hands. I wouldn't go inside until I hit that X a hundred times in a row—drawing the ire of my mother, who would often try and fail to get me to come in for dinner. When I finally did, I would dribble the ball through the house, annoying my father, who was trying to drink his scotch and watch the news in peace. After getting yelled at to "stop dribbling the damn ball in the house" enough times, I learned to spin it on my finger so I could keep it moving without making noise.

By the time I got to the ninth grade, I was good enough to play on my school's varsity team. I attended the Isidore Newman School, which was founded as a Jewish orphanage in 1903 and, over the years, was the preferred school of the city's vibrant, multigenerational Jewish community. When I attended the school in the seventies and eighties, the student population was about half Jewish and was known, mostly by people that didn't go there, as the "rich, White, Jewish school," a characterization that was hard to argue with.

My high school basketball coach was Billy Fitzgerald, a tough man of Irish descent who tried, as best he could, to knock the privilege out of a group of boys who started ahead in life as the sons of doctors, lawyers, and business owners. A towering presence in our young lives, he demanded commitment to excellence, discipline, and perseverance. His manner and coaching style were chronicled in a book by my fellow Newman graduate Michael Lewis simply titled *Coach*. Although not obvious at the time, playing for him was less about basketball and more about preparing us for the rest of our lives, which, for the vast majority of us that Fitz coached, would not include playing basketball beyond high school. In talking years later to Michael, he mentioned that Coach Fitz should open his own publishing house, given all the writing he has inspired in many of us.

But what was lost in our lived experience with Fitz was his other forms of commitment: to his intellect and, most importantly to him, to his Catholic faith. My relationship with Fitz went beyond just player and coach. I would go to his house some nights after practice and would find him sitting quietly in a reading chair with a book, his wife, Peggy, nearby or in another room tending to their four young children.

I only learned years later that this man who was facile with every intricate detail of the game of basketball was also a regular massgoer and was every bit as likely, perhaps even more likely, to read about Catholicism at night than he was, say, the teachings of the famed Indiana University basketball coach Bobby Knight. His religious devotion fascinated me at the time and was something I didn't see in my own home. I could share his love of basketball, its rigor and precision. I could take his teachings of the game and apply them on the court. I could even emulate his discipline and commitment. But his religious practice, his understanding of Catholicism, his consistent mass attendance, I couldn't have that. That was his, not mine, and I knew it at the time.

That he was doing this every day, a man who clearly was one of the two most important men in my life, quietly and without drawing attention to it, told me all I needed to know about his disposition and what mattered to him. In many ways, I wanted to please Coach even as much as I wanted to please my father and, given my father's work and travel schedule, I think I saw more of Coach Fitz in high school than I did my father, leaving an indelible impression that has never left me. It would only be decades later, when my own faith crisis came to the forefront, that I would once again seek counsel from this great man who was so much more than "just" my high school basketball coach. He was someone who gave me another close look at the meaning of faith, its shape and impact—so different from the experience of my parents, and certainly different from the one I saw in the Black churches in inner-city New Orleans. But it has stayed with me to this day.

The first game of my freshman year, we were playing against a team from just outside of New Orleans proper. The other team's parents were mostly commercial fishermen or worked at the natural gas refinery nearby. Our team's parents worked in office buildings, courtrooms, or hospitals. Even though the schools were only several miles apart, the cultures could not have been more different. I was about to find out how different.

After a timeout, one of my teammates inbounded the ball to me, and I began dribbling it up the court. As I called out a play, a complex symphony of movement we called Tennessee, I was being closely guarded by a guy who was taller and more muscular than me, which wasn't saying much. He got even closer to me as I zigzagged past half-court. Then he said something that I couldn't quite make out.

Until he said it again.

"Fucking kike."

At first, I wondered if I heard him right. The gym was loud and I was concentrating on what I was doing. I passed the ball to one of my teammates and broke away from the pass to set a screen for one of our other players. The guy who was guarding me was so close that I could feel his breath on my face.

"You're a fucking kike," he said. I quickly ran through my options and narrowed them to two: jack him in the face or ignore him. I chose the latter, largely because I wanted to remain in the game—and he was a lot bigger than I was.

After the game ended, the teams shook hands, two lines of opposing players muttering "Good game" over and over again without really meaning it. When I passed the kid who had been guarding me, he had a smug smirk on his face—really a grin that only could be described as shit-eating—framed by teenage stubble on his upper lip. I again said nothing as I walked by, touching his hand quickly while every impulse in me wanted to smash his face in.

We won the game, so on the bus ride home my teammates were celebrating, talking loudly and reliving the contest in vivid detail. I sat quietly in the front of the bus, the area designated for the underclassmen on the team. I stared out the window, looking at the oil refineries on the banks of the Mississippi River, wondering what life would be like working in one of them. And then my mind drifted back to the game and especially the guy who was guarding me.

Kike.

I wasn't sure if I should be personally insulted or just angry that anyone would call another person that. At the time, I didn't identify as Jewish or any other religion for that matter, but I was appalled nonetheless. But the more I thought about it—now and then—I wasn't the one that was being attacked, not really. Instead, I hurt for my father and especially for the little boy that he once was, running from Germany with his family, his father still freshly recovering from the emotional and physical pain of Buchenwald and all the humiliations that led up to it in Berlin.

That's how I hurt—for them, not me. But I realize now, I was/am "them." They are part of me, whether I identified that night during the game as Jewish or not. The player on the other team thought I was Jewish, assumed so perhaps based on the school I attended, the way I looked, or my last name. He attacked me, and as much as I wanted to say back then, *I'm not even Jewish, so fuck off*, it didn't matter. My relatives were, going back hundreds of years, so I was. There was no escaping that.

That night, in a sweaty Louisiana gym, in the late 1970s, I was a Jew, no matter how I identified, no matter how I resisted it. I wore it. The name, the face, the ancestry. It was all mine. There was no denying it, but I didn't fully accept it either. *Don't your parents decide what your heritage is?* I guess mine could have, perhaps should have.

But they didn't, not my mother nor my father.

But what *was* the heritage we were all avoiding? And why?

CHAPTER FOUR

THE WEILLS

Germany, 1360–1939

Kurt Weill, the author's grandfather (left), and his cousin, Kurt Weill (right), date unknown. The woman in the middle is unknown.

HERE'S WHAT I KNEW WHEN I WAS YOUNGER ABOUT THE German side of my family: We had a good run in Germany—if you call nearly six hundred years a good run—up until they/we didn't.

When I was a young boy, my father would occasionally mention that we came from a "long line of rabbis," in fact, "going back hundreds of years," he would say. At the time, this piece of family trivia didn't make much of an impression on me. I was largely indifferent to my heritage, not sure of its significance to me or to anyone else. All I could conjure up in my still-developing imagination was a group of old men with long beards and skull caps, a gathering of my ancestors in a make-believe room, discussing whatever rabbis discuss when they get together. I didn't know anything about them or fully appreciate their relevance to me.

But when my father would say something else about these forefathers, I started to understand more about him at least. "The rabbis were leaders of their communities, the ones that people would seek out advice from," and then he would point to his forehead and smile. "And they were the smart ones." Even as a little boy, I couldn't have been more than ten or eleven years old, I knew what this meant: If they were smart, and I was descended from them, then maybe I was smart. That's what my father wanted me to think—about him and about me. He was laying the foundation for how he would parent me, his only son, and even more, it was the foundation of his relationship to his own Jewishness, which was not expressed in a synagogue or celebration of the High Holidays, but rather in the mind. To him, being Jewish meant being smart—and, he was sure, we came from smart people.

Such as whom?

I wasn't sure. The only one of the German Weills that I actually met was my grandfather, Kurt Weill.

Kurt was a small man, standing five foot four and weighing just over a hundred pounds but, to me, he might as well have been a behemoth. He punched above his weight, as we say now. I had the sense though, even as a young boy, that something had happened to this man. I suspected that he had a backstory—and perhaps not a pleasant one—but I just didn't know what it was. With a thick

German accent and a brusque manner, my grandfather was not the warm cuddly type that made little children feel at ease. He wasn't one to get on the floor and play toy soldiers with me.

Our visits to Miami Beach were typical of any summer trip a young family might take. My two older sisters and I splashed around in the Atlantic Ocean, then built sandcastles on the beach while my parents—and Deborah, who typically traveled with us—looked on. We ignored the sunburn that was renewed each day of our trip, growing up in an era long before parents slathered sunscreen on their children and covered them in long-sleeved sun shirts. At midday, we would order lunch by the pool of the Fontainebleau Hotel, gorging ourselves with deli sandwiches and French fries.

But the real fascination came in the evenings when I would look around my grandfather's condominium. An antique dealer, a profession he took up later in life, he had old furniture everywhere and a vast array of clocks and mirrors hanging on the walls. He also collected rare coins and would hand me a few each time I came to visit, ones from Europe and South America. There was a collection of United States pennies, one from each year dating back to when copper pennies were first put into circulation. I still have them tucked away in a desk drawer, one of my few remaining connections to the man.

My grandfather had something else in his condominium, or rather, someone else. Gerda Meyer, also a German immigrant, lived in a back bedroom. She tended to all my grandfather's needs, and yes, she did domestic chores, but she was also something of a personal assistant. She and my grandfather spoke German to each other in front of me, usually in hushed tones. At other times, my grandfather would raise his voice. I couldn't understand the language, then or now, but even as a young boy, it was easy to tell that he was unhappy about something. Despite his rantings, Miss Meyer, as we called her, would just look away from my grandfather and smile at me, her blue eyes twinkling. She was a kind woman who, while not a love interest of my grandfather's, was certainly the most important woman in his life, someone who he simply referred to as "da Meyer."

Kurt's wife, my father's mother, passed away in 1952 of esophageal cancer. My father was nineteen when his mother died and my grandfather never remarried. He had "da Meyer" and that seemed to be enough. I think the death of his mother hardened my father's heart, making him emotionally distant, a second blow put on top of the first one, having to flee his country as a boy.

I never heard any discussion of the homeland from my grandfather, not of the Germany between the world wars, not of the Nazis, or of the horrors that got them all to America in the first place—and certainly not anything about my grandfather's time in Buchenwald. Despite this, I had a sense even back then that something bad had happened. I can see it in his face now when I conjure up an image of him, sad eyes, mouth slightly open as if he had something to say, but never did. He had a past, I knew that, something had happened, to him, to my father, to Miss Meyer. They all had that look. It wouldn't be until much later that I knew the circumstances of my father's early life, pieces that I had to put together myself with bits here and there, stories that he wasn't eager, or even willing, to share.

That was my first family lesson—emotions, we put them somewhere else. They were of very little use. We suffer in silence, a philosophy best summarized by one of my father's favorite sayings by the former UK prime minister Benjamin Disraeli, one that could have gone on his tombstone if he had been buried when he died instead of cremated: "Never complain, never explain."

Never complain, never explain.

Some families have mottoes, I suppose, even emblazon it on a family crest to be used as a guiding principle for future generations. That was ours.

In the Weill clan, there was another Kurt Weill aside from my grandfather, a renowned composer who shared not only the same name but also a bond that developed between them as both navigated the difficult circumstances the world presented when they were young adults.

When some people see my last name, they ask, usually in jest, if I am related to the composer Kurt Weill. When I respond that *Yes, I am*, these same people (usually clustered on either coast, Jewish, of German origin, or all of the above) are impressed, as if my being related to him might mean that I might be someone special, even if that relative is not a father or mother but in fact was my grandfather's first cousin. To make matters worse, in case one might wonder, I have no musical ability beyond being able to listen to music using a Spotify account—and my kids even had to show me how to do that.

Regardless, I knew certain things about Kurt Weill when I was growing up. One, he shared the same first name with my grandfather—and they were very close, as some cousins are. Two, my father, for unclear reasons, though I think mostly out of some sort of familial obligation, felt compelled to play Kurt Weill's music occasionally, usually *The Threepenny Opera*. My father made me listen to it, although I had no appreciation for the music at the time and only, perhaps, a bit more now. In my mind, related or not, famous or not, Kurt Weill's music didn't favorably compare to the Rolling Stones or the Beatles, both of whom dominated the record collection of my youth. And third, as I mentioned, we had one of the composer's violins that sat out of our reach atop a china cabinet—the only physical presence of the man, which we were not permitted to touch.

That was it—I knew nothing else. But I would come to find out later on that he played an important role in my life, one larger than I could have ever imagined when I was younger.

But I had two parents and, therefore, two sides of the family. My mother's side had a story, too, and one I knew little about when I was young.

CHAPTER FIVE

THE BURTONS

Selma, 1970s

The author's maternal grandfather, Woodson "Peck" Burton, Selma, Alabama, date unknown

GROWING UP IN A CITY LIKE NEW ORLEANS, WHERE MANY OF the people I knew were related to one another in some way and had generational roots that went back a century or more, I was often asked the question *Where is your mother from?* It was hard for some to understand that she wasn't from New Orleans and, in fact, was related to no one there. "She's from Selma," I would say, not having to add the state name to that. This was the 1970s. People knew where Selma was—and what it was.

I would wait, wondering if these folks were thinking to themselves: "Which side was she on? The right one or the wrong one?" I didn't feel a need to answer those unasked questions.

Never complain, never explain.

But I did know this. My mother left Selma at age eighteen to attend nursing school in New Orleans, a city with its own racial problems in the fifties and sixties but a place with more possibilities than Selma, perhaps a massive understatement. Turning her back on her family and religion, she sought something better for herself, something different, just like my father ultimately did under quite different circumstances. Each of my parents took a similar course of action but for vastly different reasons.

After being in New Orleans only a short time, my mother brought my father, a German immigrant—and more notably, a German Jew—to meet her parents. When my parents announced their intention to marry, my grandparents' hopes that my mother would marry a good Baptist boy from Selma and settle down in their small town were dashed.

But the union between my mother and father did happen. The life my parents built for my sisters and me in New Orleans—a complicated societal and religious environment in its own right—was the next phase of the merging of these two disparate but rich family legacies, reminding me that we are all more than just products of one parent or the other. We are products of both of our parents—and their families. I am no different.

* * *

Each summer when school let out, my mother would take the three children to Selma. During the four-hour drive from New Orleans, we spread out in the station wagon, my mother in the front, my sisters in the backseat. I was relegated to what we called the "way back," lying down next to our suitcases. Never mind seatbelts—they weren't much of a thing back then.

My father wouldn't make the trip with us. Most of the time, he would say that he had work and that "I was in charge," as we shook hands goodbye. *How could I be in charge?* I thought. I was the youngest in our family. But to my father, in his absence, the male was always in charge, even if still in elementary school. It was literally next man up. As we drove along, I would mostly just listen to the conversation. My mother would point out cotton fields and plantations as we got closer to Selma. I had studied the Civil War in school, and in fact was infatuated with Abraham Lincoln from an early age and was excited when I got to play him in the school play. I knew enough to know that he was on the right side of history, that slavery was wrong, and that it was a good thing that the South lost the War Between the States. That was all I needed to know at the time.

My grandparents' house was small but tidy, located in a lower-middle-class part of town. My grandfather had retired by that time. Before that, he was a train conductor and, as such, was gone a great deal when my mother was growing up. When he came home, sometimes the reentry was smooth—and sometimes not. My grandfather was prone to take a drink—especially on payday. When she was a little girl, my mother would isolate in her room when he was on a binge, lights off, often using a flashlight to immerse herself in her books. Throughout her life, books were her refuge, the port in the storm that characterized her early life. Soon after moving to New Orleans for nursing school, she met my father in the hospital, a doctor-nurse relationship that my father would describe as one made the "old-fashioned way." It turns out, not so old fashioned. My marriage to Jackie was the second doctor-nurse relationship in our family.

My grandparents were kind to me. My grandfather reminded me a bit of Lyndon Johnson as I think about it now, in stature, appearance, and accent. A large man, he took naps on the back porch and often I would sit in the chair as he slept, a coloring book in my lap, periodically looking up to watch him sleep, smiling to myself as he snored. Other times we would peel snap beans together as we sat on the stairs that led to the backyard, listening to a small radio that was perpetually tuned to a religious station broadcasting from Montgomery. I can still hear the preacher imploring the listeners to "*Fear the Almighty!*" or "*Be condemned to Hell!*" It all seemed a bit scary to me, as I sat peeling the snap beans, but the look on my grandfather's face never changed. He just went about the task at hand.

Aside from these memories, ones not uncommon to any child visiting their grandparents, there were other memories that were less idyllic.

My trips to Selma were the first time I heard the N-word. Now to be clear, even at a young age, I knew what the word meant. I grew up in the South after all and New Orleans was not always the epitome of racial harmony. But it was the casualness of its use in my grandparents' house that stood out to me back then, the way it was used as a descriptor in such an easy way, the same as if one was describing someone's hair color as blond or their eye color as blue. It was that casually, and carelessly, used. Just as this home environment didn't negatively influence my mother's attitudes toward Black people (and perhaps had the opposite effect), her brother was also able to overcome their parents' bigotry. My uncle Dawson had a lifelong career in the military, serving in Vietnam and elsewhere, and like many who served our country, he left behind any prejudices against other races and ethnicities when he put on the uniform and went off to war.

But it wasn't just the N-word that startled me, that made me uneasy, causing me to shift uncomfortably in whatever chair I was sitting. It was also the way Black people were referred to, certainly as "less than," but also as unworthy. When my grandfather would describe something that was a rare treat, say a good piece of steak or a fine whiskey, he would remark, holding up his fork or glass, for all to see, "Damn few White people—and no niggers at all." He meant that whatever he was enjoying at the time was an uncommon luxury—and one that Black people could/would never get to experience.

I sometimes looked at my mother when things like this were said. She just looked away most of the time, seemingly embarrassed by her mother and father, in a way that went beyond the usual embarrassment that children feel at times in the presence of their parents. But this time, the embarrassment wasn't about silly dance moves, dress, or references to how things used to be. It was about racism and, more specifically, one's parents' racism. Then, I didn't know how that affected my mother, her whole demeanor, her way of thinking. I would discover that later.

I hadn't put the pieces together yet but the clues were there, even then. She would take my sisters and me on clandestine trips to the Edmund Pettus Bridge, one of the few important historical sites in Selma, right up there with the Old Live Oak Cemetery, a Confederate burial site, or the plantation right outside of town, one of the kinds of places that the author Maurice Carlos Ruffin refers to in his novel *The American Daughters* as "a slave labor camp also known as a plantation." The trips to the bridge were kept secret by my mother from my grandparents, described only as "wanting to get the children out of the house" or "taking the kids to walk down Main Street." But to the bridge we went, so my mother's children could get a look at the real Selma, her Selma.

My mother would park the station wagon on the downtown side of the bridge and walk with us slowly up the steep incline. The sun was usually blazing hot, the summer air weighing on us as we tackled the bridge. I picked up a rock at the top the first time I was there and tossed it into the muddy Alabama River below, watching it fall the hundreds of feet down to the water. My mother played tour guide as we stood at the top, describing what had happened there in age-appropriate terms—the Black marchers, the White men on horses, the beatings that ensued. I turned away from the dizzying view of the water down below to the bridge itself, disregarding the occasional car that passed, and instead imagined the Black folks being chased and beaten by White supremacists. I blinked to get a better image in my head, or at least one that made sense.

I was too young to have experienced racism—more specifically Black hatred. I loved the only Black person I knew back then, Deborah, and I had no life experience with violence instigated by racial hatred or anything of the kind. But my mother made sure that notion stuck: "This bridge, what happened here, what it represents is unjust. Treat everyone the same. We are all God's children. That's what the Bible says."

The Bible. God.

I had only the vaguest notion of what/who she was talking about. And I wouldn't have any additional clarity any time soon on the religion issue. But I did know, especially now but also then, that part of me—my own spirituality—was shaped by those summer trips and that bridge. It was persecution, not due to skin color but rather religious affiliation, that led to my mother's rethinking of her faith, just like it was for my father on another continent. They shared that, the realization that religion had failed them—and my parents would not risk the same thing happening to their children. It posed a threat that neither was willing to confront, an understandable route that was certainly more safe but not necessarily less complex, as I would discover as I left my childhood behind.

My grandmother was a woman who stayed mostly in the kitchen and didn't say much when she was at home in Selma. I would sometimes go visit her in the kitchen, a simple setup on the back porch, but she always looked busy, only occasionally asking me to hand her a utensil or a spice of some sort. The rest of the time on that porch, I was invisible, never comfortable around my grandmother, a stern woman who was never entirely welcoming to our family. She preferred my uncle Dawson's family, I felt, because he was the ideal child, a son who catered to my grandmother's needs. My mother, on the other hand, left Selma after high school, moved to New Orleans (a decadent city in my grandparents' view) and married a man, my father, who was so different from anyone with whom they were familiar.

Usually after only a short time, I would get up and leave the stool in my grandmother's kitchen because of the heat, the metaphorical and the actual kind.

My most significant interactions with my grandmother occurred when she came to stay with us in New Orleans when my parents were out of town. As soon as she arrived, Deborah lost the easy feeling about her, the quick and broad smile, the funny banter, her disposition when she and my mother were in charge of the house. With my grandmother, Deborah had to stay guarded; I could feel the tension when I was around the two of them. I think both of them counted the days until my mother returned so that the status quo could be restored, a return to a norm that worked for all of us.

Once when my parents returned after a particularly long trip to South Africa where my father had a research collaboration, I overheard a conversation that my mother and grandmother had in the kitchen. I sat on the stairs nearby, within earshot of the two of them but out of their visual range.

"We just sat there, just the two of us, having dinner," my grandmother said, with no small amount of incredulity. My mother didn't say anything. And then my grandmother added: "Just like two people . . ." She was referring to herself and Deborah, I thought. Who else could it be?

"Uh, uh . . ." I heard my mother say, under her breath as she pulled on the refrigerator door that had a distinctive squeak when opened.

I fidgeted on the steps and processed in my ten-year-old mind what I had heard from my grandmother. *Dinner together with Deborah. Just like two people? As opposed to what?*

I stood up as quietly as possible and walked downstairs to my room, picked up my basketball—my security blanket—and lay in bed, practicing my shot, first right handed, then left, and I began to make sense of what I just heard. *But could I?*

Had I not heard similar comments in my grandparents' house about Black people, I wouldn't have thought much about what I had just heard. But my grandmother wasn't talking about *Black* people, she was talking about Deborah, a Black person, yes, but one that had a name I knew, a son I knew, a person with whom I danced to music, hugged often, and who kissed me to bed at night, usually telling me

I was something special. "Handsome, and smart, too," she would say. It was the last thing I heard those many nights.

Wanting to keep the peace, to not get into it late at night when she had just flown halfway around the world, my mother chose, at least in that moment, to gloss over her mother's comments. I didn't blame her, then or now. There was no changing a person with those views anyway. If she couldn't see Deborah as the equal of any other person, then she couldn't see. And that night in the New Orleans of the mid-1970s, there was a blind person in our house, and we all had to accept that. But she was still my grandmother and my mother's mother. My mother, and I for that matter, would be judged by our own actions, the way we each lived our lives. I learned at this early age that it wasn't necessary to own every aspect of our relatives' character. I couldn't and I wouldn't, but to be blind to it would be just that: unsighted, ignorant of a past that was as real as it was impactful.

J

DEUTSCHES REICH

REISEPASS

Nr.

NAME DES PASSINHABERS

Gerda Sara Weill geb. Philipp

~~BEGLEITET VON SEINER EHEFRAU~~

UND VON —2— KINDERN

STAATSANGEHÖRIGKEIT:

DEUTSCHES REICH

Dieser Paß enthält 32 Seiten

Nazi Germany passport of Gerda Weill,
the author's grandmother, 1939

CHAPTER SIX

"DID YOU LOSE ANY OF YOUR FAMILY IN THE HOLOCAUST?"

New Orleans, 1985

In New Orleans, the first question one is asked when meeting someone for the first time is, interestingly, about one's mother. And it goes something like this: *"Who's ya momma?"* What is really meant, but not said, is *Who* is she? Who are *her* parents? In other words, *what is your family's importance* and by extension, what is *your* importance?

I contrast this with my time spent in California. In the Bay Area, when meeting people at a dinner party or a gathering for cocktails, people would almost immediately ask, *What do you do for a living? Where did you attend college? Medical school?* It was all about what you'd done or accomplished—and perhaps, *how much money have you made?*

Not so in New Orleans. There, I am not thought of as a transplant doctor or a writer (who knows, I might not be thought of that anywhere). Instead, I'm an outsider's son. In my hometown, status is what you were born into, one's family pedigree, one's social circle. It's not my favorite aspect of the city that I love, but it is a fact of living there and one I've had to reconcile.

So for the longtime residents of the city, the connection is by family lines, who you are, not what you are, not what you have accomplished. It isn't that kind of place. But the connectedness of the place is endlessly endearing, which has kept many of us viscerally attached to it. Flaws and all, whether we natives are currently living in New Orleans or not, the connection is never lost. A common saying among the locals is "Be a New Orleanian wherever you are." No one there cares if you are a stockbroker, run a Fortune 500 company, or if you do very little at all. It was—and still is, to a significant extent—all about who your people are.

Given that my people had only recently arrived in the country—and even more recently in New Orleans—or had grown up in a notorious small Alabama town, we weren't of particular consequence, unless we forced our consequence, became something, achieved something.

How did this make me feel?

Uneasy.

That was my prevailing emotion as I went through the first part of my life.

Now, I should say up front, uneasiness does not mean unhappiness. Not necessarily. If someone asks me, *Did you have a happy childhood?* my quick and truthful answer has always been *Yes*. I grew up happy, right next to uneasy. Nowhere was that more apparent than in my relationships.

My first true love was a young woman from a prominent New Orleans family who lived in the historic Garden District section of town.

Our relationship spanned high school and part of college, eventually being upended by my ambiguous religious and social background, juxtaposed against her very clear status: that of a debutante, part of the aristocracy in New Orleans. Aside from that, in no small measure, she just might not have been that into me. I have to entertain that as a probability—with significant evidence to support that notion.

Despite that, what about the country clubs that she and many of my friends belonged to in town? I could go as their guest but would never be considered for membership. And the Mardi Gras krewes? Forget about it.

Our relationship—and the fact that it didn't last—was an early lesson. An outsider looking in, I would need to learn to forge my own path, finding a way to matter and belong. My father's feeling of Otherness affected me. In fact I inherited it, creating a sense that I/we were on an island, not part of any particular, identifiable group. It fostered an "Us against Them mentality." This mentality first germinated when my grandfather was forced to flee Nazi Germany, and continued with my father's hardscrabble quest to make it in a new country. To counter any notion of being less than worthy, my father developed an intellectual form of snobbery, castigating the lowbrow pursuits, in his view, of country club parties, society functions, and the frivolity of Mardi Gras, especially its focus on social standing.

Don't be like them, he told me. *Use your mind, strive, achieve,* he said.

And I did.

The constant trying to prove oneself over and over was passed on to me, creating an uber-competitive attitude in everything I did, especially in my career as a transplant doctor. When I tried to get a patient through a lifesaving transplant operation, I wasn't only trying to save that patient. In all likelihood—only my therapist knows for sure—I was trying to prove to the world that I belonged, that I was important, that *I* mattered, that *my father* mattered, that *we* mattered.

For me, the grind really began in college. It was time for me to put away the more decadent pursuits of my youth—hanging out in the bars, lounging by our backyard pool with my friends, my focus on basketball to the exclusion of academics. I attended Tulane University. My father was on its medical school faculty and, probably not by coincidence, it was the best school that accepted me, given my poor academic record in high school. Tulane, then and now, is a university with a large Jewish student population, most of whom are from the Northeast. I didn't fit in, either culturally or socially, and so I spent most nights alone in the library focused entirely on my pre-medical studies. That was college for me.

As a student at Tulane, aside from the pre-med requirements, I chose to take a one-on-one thesis course for an entire year with Dr. Henry Mason, a renowned Holocaust scholar, an experience that was an early inkling of my yearning to understand, in some way, what had happened to my family. I understand that now, even if that notion was buried deep in my subconscious during my college days.

"Did you lose any of your family in the Holocaust?"

The tall, dark-haired man with sad eyes peering out over his reading glasses was Dr. Mason. Though a pre-med student, I majored in political science, a rarity among my science-oriented colleagues who were also aspiring physicians. As I would come to find out during the course of the year, over coffee and casual conversation, Dr. Mason was a native of Vienna who immigrated to the United States with his Jewish father and Catholic mother in 1938. He served as an intelligence officer in the US Army during World War II, debriefing captured German soldiers. In 1952, after completing an undergraduate degree in history at Johns Hopkins University and a doctorate in political science at Columbia University, Dr. Mason began teaching at Tulane.

"I don't know . . . we, my family, we never really talked about it," I said one day soon after we first met.

"I see," Dr. Mason answered and then waited.

"I just want to know more about it, what happened, there, then." I knew my grandfather had been in a concentration camp—but which one and for how long? I was unsure. I knew that he had survived, since I was with him many times as a boy. But his real story and that of the rest of the family? I had no idea.

Dr. Mason explained to me that when students do this kind of intense Holocaust study, they focus on one aspect or the other—the efforts at dehumanizing the Jewish population, the logistics involved with the systematic deportations, or the horrors of the death camps themselves, to cite a few examples. This strategy of examining specific parts of the Holocaust made sense to me, given the complexity of the subject matter.

But I had already thought about what facet I wanted to study: the bigger-picture part.

"I want to study one specific area: How could it happen?"

Dr. Mason stood up from his desk, a wry smile on his face. "How could it happen?" he said, repeating my words. "A question for the ages. Lots to that one."

"I want to know, you know, the steps that were taken, not taken, how the Nazis got away with it." I was that sort of young man—*there must be an answer, there must be an answer*. That need to know has chased me around my whole life, especially when I was practicing medicine—and can be a real nuisance, I must say.

But this question as it pertained to the most horrific atrocity—*how could it happen?*—perplexed the world for decades, and still does. But my college-self, the one that thought there must be an answer to every question, wanted to be the one who cracked the code.

Dr. Mason and I talked some more about the logistics of the project—how often we would meet, the resources available for my research, how a paper would need to be produced at the end of the term. At the conclusion of the conversation, we shook hands. "You're going to discover a great deal, David." Then he tilted his head to one side and dug both hands into his pants pockets. "And some of it, you won't want to know." Dr. Mason couldn't have been more right. As I did my research, I encountered the big questions, the ones that were hard to comprehend—and the ones that were ultimately unanswerable. Reaching these conclusions, I had a great deal of company.

My final report was delivered to Dr. Mason on the last day of the spring semester of my junior year, nearly forty years ago. But as I read today through the words I wrote, the bound copy saved by me for some reason, the struggle to understand comes through on the pages, especially the *Why?* question: why the Nazis wanted all the Jews gone or dead, why dehumanization of the Jews was a key step in the Nazi plan, and how it was allowed to happen by those inside and outside of Germany. I also wrote about the comparison between the Holocaust, Black slavery, and nuclear war—an obsession of mine in the mid-eighties, and relevant because it too would require dehumanizing the victims in order to rationalize using a weapon of this sort ever again.

My concluding statement was one that connected me to my thoughts today, about the perilous state in which we all exist, especially the descendants of Holocaust survivors. As a college student in 1985, I wrote, "One cannot be confident about the fate of the human species after examining human behavior during the Holocaust." It was perhaps a banal statement if written by an older author, but I must confess that I was startled reading it now, as it provided an insight into a dark corner of my twenty-one-year-old mind that I didn't remember existing. Did that pessimism about human nature, what we as a species are capable of, influence the outlook I had on life? And was it the basis for my decision to become a transplant doctor—in many ways the ultimate career choice for a person that wants to change the fate of another human being—especially for someone who wanted to prove that I/we can do better? That notion certainly bears consideration.

Even more, I think that course of study back in the mid-eighties—when I was still trying to figure out who I was as a young college student—and the writings in that hundred-page document, were the first inklings that I would go on a lifelong search for my own identity, a search that now has provided some answers to the questions that I had even at an early age.

From left to right: Jackie, Ava, Hannah, and David Weill, Rosemary Beach, Florida, 2019

CHAPTER SEVEN

A FAMILY OF MY OWN

Palo Alto, California

AFTER I FINISHED MY MEDICAL TRAINING IN 1996, I MET AND then married Jackie Thompson, a devout Catholic woman from a farming community in rural Iowa. I was attracted to many things about Jackie then: her confidence, her no-nonsense disposition, the way both women and men were attracted to her. She could light up the darkest of rooms—and I figured that I would need all of that, especially given the career path upon which I was embarking.

Her religion was as much a part of her DNA as the lack of my own was a part of mine. In many ways, especially early on, our relationship with faith defined us—her close one, my ambivalent one. Religion was an unwelcome visitor to our new marriage that, like all new marriages, required an adjustment period. There were telltale signs that religion might be an awkward topic for us—from the day we were married in a Dallas hotel rather than a church, much to her parents' chagrin, to the awkward Midnight Masses during Christmas trips to Iowa, to the time we decided to send our children with my wife on Sundays to a Palo Alto Catholic church. My two daughters would eventually be baptized and confirmed at that church, but religion remained the proverbial elephant in the room. Jackie and I danced around the issue, since I didn't have the language to talk about it then. An honest assessment would be that, early on, religion was a source of conflict at times, a wedge that created unwanted distance.

But I stood firmly unaffiliated with any type of formal religion. My faith, my spiritual experience, was at the hospital, where I did rounds nearly every Sunday morning while my wife and two young daughters sat in the pews. My patients provided all the miracles that I would ever need, I thought—and I had a role in providing those miracles, or so I arrogantly concluded. I rationalized that I could do more good in the hospital than I could being with my family at church, but I now see the folly in that thinking. Why was I in the hospital most Sundays when my daughters and wife sat without me in church, even if I didn't quite feel like it was *my* church? It was the separation of Sunday experiences that never felt right to me, that in fact made me feel not just alienated from my family but from everyone who had a place to go on Sundays—or Saturdays. I was certainly aware that only a small fraction of people regularly availed themselves of that religious opportunity, but knowing they could if they wanted to, at least in my view, gave them a leg up on me. I had the choice about whether or not to attend a church or a synagogue. But "none of the above" was my default position.

When she was young, my oldest daughter, Hannah, would ask why I didn't go to church with the rest of the family on Sundays. "Work," I said, just like my father told me when he couldn't, or didn't want to, do something with the family. As she got a bit older, I told her instead, in an effort of some transparency at least, "I'm not

Catholic." She was around ten years old at that point, and she looked at me, eyes squinting, brow furrowed in deep thought, one of my daughter's most endearing childhood facial expressions. "What are you then?"

What am I then?

Good question, kid.

All this didn't mean that I was entirely devoid of religious curiosity. I periodically looked over the fence to see what was there. The most profound instance of this voyeurism happened in September 2005 soon after Hurricane Katrina hit New Orleans. Watching the coverage on television from our home in California, thousands of miles away in comfort and safety, was crushing, reminding me of the period after 9/11 when none of us could shut off the news.

In the days after the storm, my hometown was in turmoil, its people in despair, neighborhoods washed away. Buildings that had been there for centuries burned to the ground. The storm affected me viscerally, as it did so many others who loved the city. I needed to understand what happened on a whole other level and though I didn't have any formal religion in my life, I turned to the Bible.

Like most things I wanted to understand, I went all in. I decided to read the Bible all the way through, both the Old and New Testaments, using a daily Bible reader that guided me through the entire Bible in a year. Each morning, I read the assigned passages for that day right when I got up, sometimes highlighting certain sections or writing notes in the book margins.

I took great interest in what I was reading for those twenty or so minutes each day and was amazed, as many have been over the last two thousand years, how little of humankind's struggles have changed. I was comforted by the notion that what I was grappling with in my own life was much the same as what people faced hundreds and even thousands of years ago. So, each day for a year, I read until I finished the entire Bible. And then I did it again the next year. And the year after. That was my Katrina experience.

I read the Bible faithfully, yes, but this specific relationship to religion, done my way, on my own timetable, still didn't quell my uneasiness with religion nor did it allow me to answer the questions my young daughters continued to ask me: *Why don't you come to church with us? Are you Catholic? What religion are you?* I didn't have an easy answer, a way to explain something so complicated to two young girls who just wanted to be together as a family in church, who saw other families perform that very same ritual together each Sunday. I couldn't explain to them that I too had experience with religion, going back to well before they were born, but not the kind they were accustomed to. My cathedral was a hospital filled with sick people, not a church or synagogue filled with worshippers. My religion was helping people survive after a transplant. It was my religion before I had any. It was my identity. But more than that, it was my everything.

CHAPTER EIGHT

TRANSPLANT: MY RELIGION BEFORE I HAD ONE

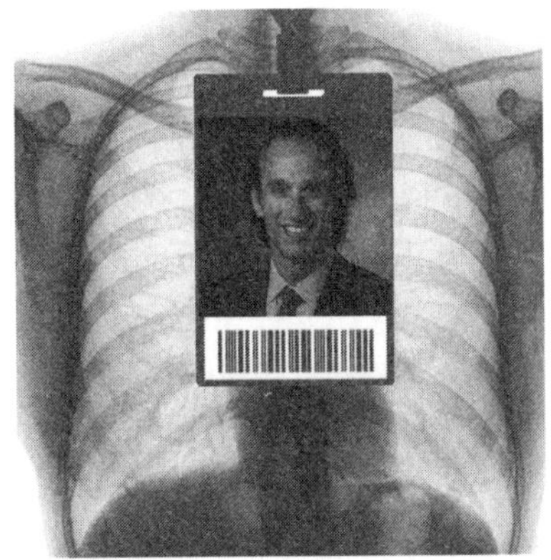

The author, Stanford, California, 2011

WHILE ON A FIRST DATE IN THE MID-1990S:

Her question: *What religion are you?*

My answer: *Transplantation.*

Uncomfortable laughter.

There wasn't a second date.

As a transplant doctor, I wrote in my memoir *Exhale* that my mission was to save everyone, including my father, who developed hepatitis C and needed a liver transplant to survive. But all along I was trying to save myself, to feel wanted, to be a hero. My career thus became a rescue mission—of my father the Jew, his people, and other people like him. I couldn't be there to help save the Holocaust victims, but I sure as hell could save my father and patients like him. A storybook reason to enter the healing arts? Perhaps not, but it was my reason and the way I practiced medicine was influenced by where I came from, how I was hatched.

For some people, career choice is influenced by the usual factors one uses to assess the direction of their professional life: interest, money, the desire to make a difference in other people's lives or, as the saying goes, the ability to "dent the universe."

My career gave me all these things—and more. I was fascinated by the prospect of changing the direction of a patient's life with a transplant—snatching life from death—or, as a former colleague used to say, immodestly, "Pushing away the hand of Jesus."

I invested my whole being in building my career as a transplant doctor, rising to the pinnacle of my profession by becoming the head of the Stanford lung transplant program—and was paid handsomely to do so, though money was never my main motivating factor. Instead, this quest was about other things, all rooted I believe in a sense of constantly needing to prove myself, and manifested by uber-competitiveness and addiction to the profound appreciation and respect given to me by my patients and colleagues. I would on occasion clash with my coworkers when I considered them not committed enough to the "cause." And most importantly, the job was a way to prove to my father that I was worthy of his affection, yes, but also his respect. But not only that *I* deserved respect, but that *we* did—him, me, and our Jewish ancestors before us.

This take-no-prisoners approach worked well, until late in my career when I should have been formulating an elegant exit strategy.

Instead, I reached a crisis point, when I became disillusioned with the practice of modern medicine, with all its bureaucratic inefficiencies, political infighting, and soulless indignities. Most importantly, my empathy depletion, after watching patients of mine die in this high-stakes practice of medicine, had me looking for an off ramp. The road to the exit was a bumpy one, a story I tell in *Exhale*. But my career problem turned into a full-blown life crisis when my father died, leaving me without the guiding influence that I relied on up until his death.

As much as my career brought me—purpose, confidence, a way to provide for my family—the hospital life didn't provide any cover for my uncertainty about religion and the existence of a higher spiritual being. In fact, my transplant patients provided me a nearly daily reminder of these forces that were unresolved for me.

I practiced transplant medicine both in the South and on the West Coast. In the South, the practice of religion, belief in God, and regular reference to It, is more common than in other parts of the country. When I worked at the University of Alabama–Birmingham early in my career, our team performed a double lung transplant on a nineteen-year-old cystic fibrosis patient who was so sick that we needed to place her on a mechanical ventilator while we waited for a pair of donor lungs to become available. I visited the young woman right before we intubated her and told her the plan: We would sedate and ventilate her, stabilize her vital signs, and search for a new set of lungs. She was gasping for air, her oxygen saturation in the low eighties—I knew we needed to move fast.

"Alright, here we go, Susan. When you wake up, you'll have new lungs and be breathing like a champ." This was my typical attitude when I took care of patients like this: extreme confidence (yes, some would call it arrogance), never letting doubt creep in to either the patient's mind or mine. But even through her struggles, she stayed calm. Her eyes never revealed a hint of concern. She touched my white coat and gently pulled me in. "The Lord will provide for me. I'm in His hands now."

My younger self wasn't buying that. In my own unevolved way, I thought she wasn't in God's or anyone else's hands. She was in mine. I practiced medicine that way, which made me feel wholly responsible for all outcomes, both good and bad. Back then, when things turned out well, *I* saved someone's life. That's a good feeling, if that's how one looks at things. But more than that, it's like a drug—you want more and more of it. But that way of thinking had a flip side: When a patient died, that was also my fault. That's a bad feeling. If you had hundreds of those experiences over a twenty-five-year career, you'd soon be looking for another line of work—and I eventually did.

After I intubated Susan and got her stabilized, I left the ICU to talk with her parents. They were dressed in jeans and rumpled sweatshirts—I could immediately tell they had been up all night. There was a pizza box nearby and several empty water bottles. When I walked up, they stood, eager to hear what I had to say about their daughter.

"She's stable," I said and I could see both of them relax by several degrees, their body language obvious. Then I went to my standard language: "We're looking for lungs. Right now. We'll find her some . . . get it done." I said this to them, and to many others, even though I knew the clock was running and there was less than an even chance we would even find lungs for her, much less get her through the difficult surgery. Regardless, I thought it was my job to instill this hope, this belief for these anxious parents.

But I didn't need to. They already had it. Not belief in me, but in something greater. "We have been praying all night, doctor. If it's God's will, it'll happen," Susan's father said, squeezing his wife's hand as he talked.

God's will. God's will? That question was all I could think about as I walked down the hospital hallway to my office, one of the many times during my career that I had to consider this very question. *What is God's will? To save this young woman? Not to save her?* Then even: *What about my other patients?* On my more sullen days, I even went further: *The Holocaust. God's will?* To wipe out not only six million people, but an attempt to wipe out *a people.*

But there were other days. On several occasions, patients told me that they not only believed in God, but saw Him/Her/It, or at least a representation of a spiritual force of some kind, when it looked as though death was imminent. To me that was evidence, scientific and medical evidence, the kind I cherished. I had proof! Or at the very least a secondhand account of it.

A middle-aged man who nearly died in the ICU—twice—after a lung transplant while I was at Stanford told me he saw "this beautiful light that was warm and comforting," a feeling of total serenity he said he never found in his terrestrial life. Or there was the young man who had a near-death experience while waiting for a combined heart-lung transplant who came back to life after the ICU team scrambled to save him with powerful medications and various other measures. When he woke up, the first thing out of his mouth was, "Dr. Weill, it was so beautiful. Everyone was there. My grandparents, a friend of mine who died in an accident, even my first dog." At the time, I sort of believed him and sort of didn't. Was it the powerful medications? The narcotics? Was all of this a hallucination?

But back then, I was looking for any explanation, ideally a scientific one, anything other than an Almighty force. I had no context for believing in such things, but it was constantly all around me in the hospital. The patients we saved but shouldn't have been able to, given how sick they were, or the ones we lost who by all rights should have lived. None of it made real sense to me. Something was going on out there. I knew that. I just didn't know what—and had no religious context in which to process it. But that didn't mean it wasn't happening and that I wasn't noticing.

But my conclusion from the hospital about religion was easy to summarize, and perhaps a bit surprising given my background: It didn't seem scientifically plausible that there was no God. It just didn't.

As it turns out, I am not that different from the majority of physicians.

Inquiries into the religious beliefs, or the lack thereof, among US scientists date back to a landmark 1916 survey by psychologist James Leuba that documented widespread disbelief. Leuba found that only 40 percent of scientists believed in a personal God, 15 percent were uncertain, and 45 percent were nonbelievers. Surveys published in *Nature* in 1997 and 1998, showed that little had changed since 1916, with only 39 percent of all scientists declaring a personal belief in God. Belief among "leading" scientists, however, defined in this case as members of the National Academy of Sciences, was far lower: only 7 percent in 1998. Curiously, among scientists, mathematicians were the most likely to believe in God, and biologists the least likely.

Christian, Mormon, and Buddhist doctors were the most likely to say "my religious beliefs influence my practice of medicine." Jewish and Hindu physicians were the least likely. Not surprisingly, physicians from the South and the Midwest were more religious than those from the East and the West.

In 2005, a survey of two thousand physicians by the University of Chicago found that 76 percent of doctors believed in God and 59 percent believed in some sort of afterlife. The survey found that 90 percent of doctors in the United States attended religious services at least occasionally, compared to 81 percent of adults in the general population. Fifty-five percent of doctors said their religious beliefs influenced how they practice medicine.

The researchers commented that their results were not anticipated. The results surprised me, too. In general, religious belief tends to decrease as education and income levels increase, yet doctors are highly educated and well compensated, and physicians seem to be religious believers at a higher rate than the general population. The results also differed radically from ninety years of studies showing that only a minority of scientists (excluding physicians) believes in God or an afterlife.

"We did not think physicians were nearly this religious," said study author Farr Curlin, MD, instructor in the Department of Medicine and a member of the MacLean Center for Clinical Medical Ethics at the University of Chicago. "We suspect that people who combine an aptitude for science with an interest in religion and an affinity for public service are particularly attracted to medicine. The responsibility to care for those who are suffering, and the rewards of helping those in need, resonate throughout most religious traditions."

Although physicians have extensive training in biology, the study by Curlin and colleagues paints a very different picture, showing high levels of belief—perhaps because physicians regularly have to deal with, and talk about, issues surrounding life and death. In my view, having been in these situations many times, witnessing near-death experiences makes one more likely to accept God and the existence of an afterlife. Our patients teach us that without even necessarily trying to do so.

As I look back at it now, despite the lack of formal religion in my early life, the practice of medicine was the anchor of my faith, my secular version of spirituality. It was all there, having all the components of a faith-based existence: life, death, morality, ethics, gratitude, helping others that need help. The hospital provided that to me, every day when I walked in the door, if only I could keep my eyes open to what was so apparent inside those four walls.

But was that kind of religion ever going to be enough for me, the kind which is established experientially in the service of others? Could it provide a replacement for a formal religion that I could call my own, one that I could say by name at a dinner party when meeting someone for the first time? Or would I have to search for one of the commonly accepted faiths, one that was unrelated to what was happening in the hospital?

If medicine indirectly taught me things about religion, what other experiences did so more directly?

CHAPTER NINE

A TRIP TO THE HOLY LAND

Israel, 2011

Tel Aviv, 2011

"I'M . . . WE . . . I MEAN, MY FATHER IS JEWISH."

The group sitting across from me was confused. It was the first day of an American Israel Public Affairs Committee–sponsored trip to Israel, and we had stopped for lunch in Old Jaffa. Over hummus and falafel, the group chitchatted, trying to get to know one another, comparing experiences, backgrounds, and yes, our religion résumés.

Along with a close friend of mine, Tim Ranzetta, I had decided to visit Israel in 2011, something I had wanted to do for years. Tim and I had talked about it for months as we rode our bikes together in the hills west of Palo Alto, discussing what we wanted to see and what to expect when we got there. Tim is a cradle Catholic but naturally curious about nearly everything, including his own religion as well as the Jewish faith and the geopolitics of Israel.

And my interest in going? Unclear at the time. Was it the political science major in me wanting to see the place firsthand? Or was it an attempt at comparison shopping at the crossroads of all the main faiths? The Church of the Holy Sepulchre one day, the Temple Mount the next, then the Dome of the Rock.

After our travel plans were finalized, I told my father, who had never been to Israel, that I was going. Already thinking of a second trip there, even before my first, I probed my father's interest in traveling to Israel someday, perhaps with me. "Maybe after I get a lay of the land, we could go together . . ." I suggested during one of our daily phone calls. I thought just then of the 1990 trip to Berlin that we had planned together, only to have my father bow out due to work obligations. Alone in Berlin, I walked around for a few days in the rain, knocking pieces of the Berlin Wall off with the pointed end of my umbrella, understanding that the city was the place of my father's birth but unable at the time to access the full scope of what the place meant to my family—and to me.

To the question of visiting Israel one day with me, my father said, "I don't know. I don't have a ton of interest in going there." Which in my father's vernacular meant he had no interest in going there. I was surprised—and not surprised. He did not naturally gravitate toward religion—I knew that—but I hoped, as he entered the final stretch of his life, that he might become more interested in his own religion, or at least some form of spirituality.

But he wasn't, so off I went to Israel without him, undeterred.

"So you're Jewish, right?" A few couples traveling with us stared at me.

Here we go again. Would this question ever leave me?

"Well, it's complicated . . ." My stock answer when I didn't want to get into it.

But Tim rescued me. "He's exploring—seeing what's out there."

"I see," a gray-haired man from Los Angeles said, adjusting his blue Dodgers cap. And then his wife said more bluntly, staring at me through oversized dark sunglasses, "So you two are a couple: the Catholic and the Maybe Jew."

Tim laughed. "Something like that but both of us are happily married—to other people."

That's how it went the whole trip. When we visited Haifa, the West Bank, the Sea of Galilee, Tim and I were a religious form of the Odd Couple, which might have been more accurately described as the Outside Couple, especially among a group of Zionist Americans, most of whom had visited Israel several times. But for me, the whole trip was dipping my toe in the water, standing off to the side checking things out while the less conflicted, less ambiguous among us went on with their lives.

Israel fascinated me, all of it: the religious sites certainly but also the culture, the people, even the landscape. But ironically, one of the more meaningful moments occurred when it came time to leave the country and return to the United States.

* * *

"Why don't you speak Hebrew?"

I was in a small room near Security at the Ben Gurion Airport in Tel Aviv. I had been selected for additional screening, buying me some quality time with the twitchy young man in an IDF uniform who stood before me.

The man asking me the question couldn't have been much older than twenty. He was an intense guy who apparently took his job seriously for reasons I could understand. What he didn't know was that it was just as likely for me to speak Swahili as it was Hebrew. I tried to explain.

"I'm not Jewish, so I never would have learned Hebrew." *Except the word* schtup, I thought just then, a hint of a smile creasing my face. I kept that one to myself. As my mother said to me (often) when I was a boy, *this was neither the time nor the place . . .*

He looked at my passport again. "Weill." He pronounced my last name the German way, with a V sound at the beginning. "A Jewish name."

Oh, brother.

"My father was from Germany, his family left because of the war."

"Because he was Jewish?"

"Yes. His family was." I was hedging for some reason.

"But you say you're not Jewish?"

Here we go again.

"I'm not. My mother is Baptist." This confused my young friend.

"Why did your father marry her, a non-Jew?"

You'll have to ask him, I wanted to say. *I wasn't around for that decision.*

This went on for four hours. Yep, four hours. The contents of my suitcase were strewn across a large cardboard table, a metaphor for the examination of my religious life, first by this young man, then by an older gentleman who came in later, a tall, bald man, who menaced me with questions that became increasingly pointed.

"You say you're not Jewish," the Kojak look-alike began and then paused for a moment. "Why not?" I didn't take this as a rhetorical question. He seemed like he genuinely wanted to know.

I started to give my stock answer—*how much time do you have?*—but we had already been at this for a few hours and I was afraid that he would answer, *All the time in the world.*

After more questions in this vein—*Why did you come to Israel? Where did you visit? Who did you travel with?*—and an ever-increasing amount of frustration on my part, the men said I could go and handed me back my passport. Just like that. I collected the contents from my suitcase, carefully repacked them, and wheeled my luggage back out into the terminal.

Tim was waiting patiently for me at an airport bar, on his second beer as I walked up. I eyed his glass, desperately wanting a drink, or maybe, several.

"What was that all about?" he asked.

"Oh, you know, the usual: religion," I answered, shaking my head at what just happened.

Tim smiled, knowing the running debate that had been going on inside my head since a young age. "You better clean that shit up, get your story straight."

I laughed. "Yeah, that's occurred to me."

I thought about ordering a drink, but then looked at my watch. We needed to get to the gate. Apparently the five-hour lead time we gave ourselves was just barely going to be sufficient—but plenty of time to be reminded once again of my struggle with religion, appropriately enough brought to the surface by my bumpy departure from the birthplace of all religions.

As I settled into my seat and the plane began to rumble down the runway, I thought Tim was right: I would have to eventually get my story straight.

But what was really happening? Why had I visited Israel, as the young security official at the airport had asked? I look back now and think I was flirting, seeing all the religions in their birthplace, with the only question left unanswered: Which turn do I make in the Old City?

It would take more than a trip to Israel to cause me to finally address the religion question once and for all. It would take a full-blown crisis, a life-shattering experience that would finally push me toward a new awakening.

CHAPTER TEN

CRISIS

Palo Alto, 2015

The author at his baptism in Palo Alto, California, 2015

I LOVED TRANSPLANTATION, AND MOSTLY IT LOVED ME. I didn't just have a fervent zeal for my work; at times my passion rose to the level of a religious practice—and an extreme one at that. I experienced the profound joys of seeing life snatched from death, patients returning to their families whole and healthy, getting the chance at a second life that they—and I—dreamed about. It was a renewal for my patients, yes, but it was a daily renewal for me as well.

The whole transplant experience, my role in it, the way my patients impacted me was my primary source of self-worth, something that at times has been difficult to consider a strength of mine.

But then a crisis occurred, the simultaneous unraveling of my carefully crafted career and my father's death, that shook me to my core. The experience made me question everything, including for the first time in my life, existential questions: *What was my real purpose in life? What was the point of it all?* I now knew what despair really meant, how it felt emotionally and physically, what it could do to a person, what it had done to me. I was living in a dream state—or, better described, a nightmare state, going through the motions with my wife and two young daughters, exercising each day for hours without purpose or rationality, unable to know when to stop, then eager to hit the wine bottle as soon as I got home.

And that was the emotional pain. Next came chronic pain, a physical set of symptoms that almost certainly were a reflection of what was happening inside of me. For months, and then it would turn out to be years, I saw doctors who gave me only vague theories about what was happening. "Your body is physically expressing your emotional pain," I was told over and over by pain psychologists. I got treatment for the physical and emotional parts, a great deal of it, but the symptoms wore on.

I have never contemplated death by suicide in my life and didn't then either. In fact when I heard about death by suicide prior to that period in my life, I thought all the usual things "happy" people think: *How could they do that to the people they left behind? Wasn't there another way? How could they?* I wondered, given that I had spent my entire professional life caring for people that desperately wanted to live. Since that period ten years ago, I don't think that way anymore. Instead I think, *I get it—but dying that way?* It's just not for me.

I needed to find something else though. That much was clear.

My (First) Awakening

In my moment of crisis, I did what many have done before me: I turned to religion. But I didn't want more of the solitary, Bible-reading experience that I had in the past. Instead I had a strong desire to practice a formal religion. I wanted to have that anchor when I needed it most, to have something I could call my own, a vessel of sorts that I could use to sail away from my despair.

But for me, the real question was *Which religion?* Jewish, like my father, even though he didn't practice it or believe in religion at all? Baptist, like my mother, who had also turned her back on her religion? As she often said, how can parishioners listen to a sermon on Sunday about how all of us are God's children, only to see some in the pews turn firehoses on Black people Monday through Saturday?

Or what about being Catholic, like my wife and two daughters?

Those seemed to be the choices in front of me. I was a free agent when it came to religion, and I could weigh the pros and cons of each and pick one.

If someone had asked me back then, *what do Catholics believe?* I would have been hard pressed to provide an answer. Or if asked, *What characterizes a Catholic? What are "they" like?* I would have had a difficult time even generalizing. But what I did know was something that mattered to me—and mattered a great deal. My family was Catholic. That much I knew.

The family option won out.

I chose Catholicism and immersed myself in learning all I could about it, going to classes at the church every Monday night for nearly a year. Jackie neither encouraged nor discouraged me from doing so. There was no pressure of any kind. The only comment she did have was that "you must really want to do this if you are willing to give up a whole season of Monday Night Football." True indeed.

The first RCIA (Rite of Christian Initiation of Adults) class met on the second Monday of September in 2015. I finished my afternoon rounds at the hospital, then went home to grab a quick bite to eat before the six o'clock meeting. The class was directed by a couple, Bob and Sue, from the community who had been volunteer teachers for years to help new, or lapsed, Catholics learn the ins and outs of the religion.

That first night, we sat around cardboard tables that were pushed together and introduced ourselves. Aside from Father Matt, the priest in charge of the RCIA program, and the deacon of the church, Patrick, the students were three couples and me. Bob and Sue told us the details of a weekly agenda that included a discussion of Catholic topics, such as communion, baptism, confession, the Holy Sacrament, and various other subjects. We were assigned readings, homework as it were, that was expected to inform the discussion each week. I noticed right away that the teachings would be of a traditional sort—there wouldn't be a "Controversies in Catholicism" section that might cover, say, gay marriage, or abortion, or—yikes—the issue of whether the Church should be reformed after the revelation of child molestation among a relatively small group of priests. I don't know if I really suspected these matters to come up, but I would have welcomed discussion of them, and of the other less flattering aspects of Catholicism that were in the news. I needed to know what I was getting into.

But first, introductions.

"Why don't you all tell us a little bit about yourself and why you chose to go through the RCIA process?" asked Sue, as a way to break the ice. My heart jumped a bit. This was the part I didn't look forward to, having to explain my religious background and, well, why I was there, since I was still trying to work that out for myself.

Sue, question for you, how much time do you want to devote to this? The whole three hours or something less than that? I let that question go unasked and waited for the others to go first.

Cassandra and Michael were planning to get married in the spring. Both were wedding-magazine gorgeous—dark-skinned, with beautiful brown eyes—and shared a special kind of magnetism that took me aback. I listened closely as they spoke: They were Brazilian, both from prominent families, Stanford grads. Cassandra was Catholic and Michael was Protestant, they said, finishing each other's sentences. The glow of their new relationship was unmistakable, and I can't deny that I was a bit jealous. Their lives were all in front of them: the children that were sure to come, birthday parties, job promotions, setbacks, fights even, and makeups. Cassandra's parents were devout Catholics and wanted the couple to marry in a church. Michael and his family weren't much on religion, attending church only on Christmas Eve (most of the time) and Easter (nearly always). So here they sat, as they would faithfully for the next nine months, to spiritually tidy up for the Big Day.

Next were Stuart and Cindy, who were devoutly Catholic, they said, but wanted a refresher course. Both thought there was no better way to accomplish that mission than to take the WHOLE RCIA COURSE! (The caps and exclamation mark were theirs.) I don't remember anything else they said, still digesting their whole refresher-course strategy, with Monday Night Football as a sure casualty of this approach—at least in my mind, if not theirs.

Finally, there were Brian and Nicole, married with three kids under five years old, dark circles under their eyes, speaking in mumbled sentence fragments, exhausted in only a way that parents with little children can be. Decimated, really. I pictured their household as they spoke, plastic toys littering every inch of floor space, a rescue dog with a bladder problem, half-eaten pieces of toast and scrambled eggs on the kitchen counter. "We're lapsed Catholics," Brian said, as Nicole stared off into space. "We want to do better . . . for the kids," he said unenthusiastically. Seemed to me this couple was already doing plenty.

And then it was my turn.

In a split-second decision, I decided to take the easy way out. I didn't have it in me to go through my whole religious backstory.

"My wife, my two daughters are Catholic. I want to become Catholic," I said, still somewhat surprised at the words coming out of my mouth. My father was dead but, as I spoke, I was sure he could hear me, sitting next to me with a look of abject skepticism on his face. If my pursuit of formal religion surprised me, it would have floored him, perhaps based not so much on which religion I had chosen, but rather that I had chosen any at all.

I stopped right there, but Sue wasn't having any of it.

"So you want to convert to Catholicism?" Sue asked, desperately trying to fit me into a box with which she was familiar.

I paused. "Not converting because that would mean I'm converting *from* something. I'm nothing." Then I smiled, "As it relates to religion, that is." I welcomed the laughter in the room, as the group exhaled. Then I waved my hand. "It's complicated." A few bits of nervous laughter. They'd get used to me. We would have nine months. No need to spill all of it tonight.

* * *

The next few Monday sessions were highly enlightening. I learned what the little Communion wafer represented, what drinking the wine meant (and not why I usually drank wine), how to give Confession. I memorized the Lord's Prayer and practiced it in front of my bathroom mirror. I read the assignments on our living room couch in Palo Alto, reading glasses perched at the end of my nose, yellow highlighter in hand. "It's not a test, you know," Jackie said. I stopped reading and smiled back at her. "For you it isn't." We had similar discussions many times in other contexts. One of my weaknesses, which admittedly could appear as a strength, was that for me everything was a test. And it was going to be no different as I took up a religion for the first time.

But aside from all the reading and the classes, I wanted something else. I think it was the "why" that I was missing. *Why formal religion? Why Catholicism? What was the imperative?*

To delve deeper, I asked Father Matt if I could meet with him one-on-one. "Sure," he said after one of our Monday sessions. He didn't bother to ask why I wanted to see him. I guess in his line of work, he would just let folks get to whatever matter they wanted to talk about in due course.

"How about Thursday?" I suggested.

Father Matt shook his head. "The Patriots play on Thursday night."

"Good to know you're protecting time for the important things in life, Father," I said, not really joking. "How about Wednesday?"

"You're on," he said.

"One more question: Why aren't you a Saints fan? Would seem to fit into your day job, don't you think?"

"The Patriots, my friend. I'm a Boston sports fan, through and through. Ever since seminary school there."

"Well, you have a decent quarterback," I said referring to Tom Brady.

"That we do. See you on Wednesday."

I pulled into the church parking lot at the appointed time. Father Matt lived in a dormitory-style building that sat behind the church. He met me in civilian clothes, which took me by surprise, sort of like when the paparazzi catch your favorite actor unshaven in baggy clothes and house slippers, a to-go coffee cup in their hand.

I followed Matt to his living quarters, which was a simple accommodation: a bedroom with a single bed and a desk with a reading light and a Bible on top. I looked around the room while we settled in. A rendering of Jesus Christ was the only wall hanging, perched directly above the bed's headboard. The other room had a couch and a couple of chairs facing it and not much else. Matt took a seat on one of the chairs and I sat opposite him on the couch. There was a bookcase filled with books, mostly about philosophy and Catholicism, sprinkled in with some military history titles. One thing, though, was missing, I thought: a television. *Where did he watch his Patriots?*

"How do you think the RCIA process is going for you?" Matt asked. People at the church were less likely to call RCIA "classes" or a "course," but instead usually referred to it as a "process." It made sense—it *was* a process, a slow, methodical study of a religion that was thousands of years old, a journey added by reading and conversation. In other words, the complete opposite of my day job that required I jolt out of bed while it was still dark and the whole house was asleep, then go a thousand miles an hour, making a few hundred decisions that might mean the difference between life and death for my patients. And when all that was done, I would race home in time for dinner with the family.

"Well, learning a lot," I said. "It's all new to me," an understatement if there ever was one.

"I've gathered, but that's a good thing, it will keep you interested."

I nodded in agreement but wanted to get right to what I wanted to talk with him about. I looked up at the ceiling. "I am going through a rough . . . um . . . you know . . . a difficult time."

I glanced over at Father Matt. He was looking straight at me but didn't look like he planned on saying anything. I gathered that he was a professional listener, accustomed to letting others talk, so I plowed ahead. "My father died, and I'm not doing so well with that." I paused in case he wanted to say something: *I'm sorry, that sucks,* or even *God had a different plan for him than what was here on Earth.* But he let me keep talking. "And my job is not going so well. I'm fighting with some people at work—and I can't stand to watch anyone die anymore." Then I laughed abruptly, nearly hysterical laughter that came out much louder than I anticipated. "Which is definitely a feature of my job that I can't change."

"I know what you mean," Matt said with a sly smile.

"I suspect so." I paused. I wasn't sure if I wanted to tell Father Matt about the chronic pain syndrome that I had developed soon after my father died, a maddening condition that was completely refractory to the medical or psychological therapy I had been receiving. I decided to go for it. "And I have pain all the time . . ." I waved my hand through the air dismissively, trying to diminish the impact my body's full revolt against itself had on my psyche, world attitude, mood, everything. It was something that could certainly not be ignored and definitely not dismissed, as much as I tried to do just that.

We sat for a few minutes in complete silence, the priest and I, a counseling session that for me was as unlikely a few months ago as, say, an encounter with a space alien or tea with a mountain lion. But there I sat.

Finally, Matt broke the silence. "Have you thought much about the word 'crisis'?"

"Lately? Yes," I said, smiling reflexively, a mask that I wore to diminish what was going on inside of me. "But before . . . I usually associated the word 'crisis' with someone else."

Matt tilted his head back. "Welcome to the human race. Glad to have you." He sat more forward in his chair. I suspected he was about to do some priest stuff. "Crisis in the eyes of the Church means a time of decision or transition. In Catholicism, it doesn't have the negative connotation it has in the general lexicon. Crisis is less tragedy and more opportunity."

"Kinda feels like tragedy from where I sit," I continued, genuinely interested in this new way of looking at life's challenges. "We should embrace crises then?"

"If not embrace, then understand that they are inevitable. That crises are simply a time to make some decisions, to move to something else . . . something better."

I ran that around my brain for a few moments. "And you believe that?"

"I do," Matt smiled. I had to ask—true beliefs, acceptance of the human condition, understanding that difficult times are meant to teach, to improve oneself—these concepts were all foreign to me. In my younger days, I didn't have any of these lessons taught to me by priests, rabbis, or imams. My only understanding of Crisis—gleaned from coaches, my father, and medical mentors—was do better, try harder, think one's way out of any tough situation. That strategy, while perhaps a fine one in my previous life, wasn't going to work this time, of that I was sure. I just needed Father Matt to tell me there was another way, a more evolved way, a better way than the one with which I was most comfortable.

Father Matt and I talked further about my religious upbringing, my parents, Jackie and the kids. I had to ask him about how he squared his love of the New England Patriots with his having no television. "That's the easiest one you've asked all day. I go to the Old Pro and watch." The Old Pro was a sports bar in downtown Palo Alto frequented by Stanford students, tech entrepreneurs, and really anyone who loved sports—and drinks.

"Do you, you know . . ." I made a drinking motion with my hand. "Have a couple of beers?"

Matt made the same drinking motion back to me, I'm not sure if in jest or not. "Yes. It's a sports bar, so I have drinks."

"I just didn't know if it was cool . . . you know . . . for priests to drink."

"You haven't heard of Irish Catholics, or Catholic weddings . . . yeah, we drink . . . especially when the Patriots play."

Now we were on familiar territory. "Good. That makes me feel better with this whole Catholicism thing."

"Glad I could help." The sly smile had returned to Matt's face.

After a bit more chitchat, I got up and walked to the door. It was time to go—I had been there for nearly two hours. As I turned to say goodbye, Matt put out his hand. I looked at it. "Can I give you a hug?" Then I held up my hand. "Just a basic man hug?"

"Yeah we do that, too." He gave me an embrace, squeezed my shoulder, and patted my back.

"Thanks for the conversation, Father. I'd like to do it again sometime."

Matt smiled. "We never close."

He shut the door behind me and I stood there for a second. *That was helpful,* I said to myself, somewhat surprised. *Really helpful.* I nearly skipped down the hall and out the door to the outside where my whole world waited, the good and the bad. But now, this time, I felt better, more prepared to confront it. *Was that the purpose of religion? The Why?*

Perhaps so.

In the spring, I was baptized in front of my wife and daughters, friends, and the entire congregation in Palo Alto. Following that, my family and I went to church each Sunday in California, a happy unit, just like all the others in the congregation. We sat together, said the Lord's Prayer and Family Prayer together. I learned how to make the sign of the cross over my chest—quickly, reflexively, without a second thought—just like all the veteran Catholics standing next to me. My daughters watched me cross myself during services and smiled. It made me happy that my being there made them happy. These were Sunday mornings that I'll never forget. How could I? My kids and wife were healthy and safe. We were all spiritually connected. I felt younger too, optimistic that things were straightening out for me.

For the first time in my life, when someone asked me what religion I was, I could answer the question without stammering. *Catholic,* I replied. *Catholic.*

I was content—until I had a conversation with my book publicist a few years later.

CHAPTER ELEVEN

"YOU'RE JEWISH"

New Orleans, 2020

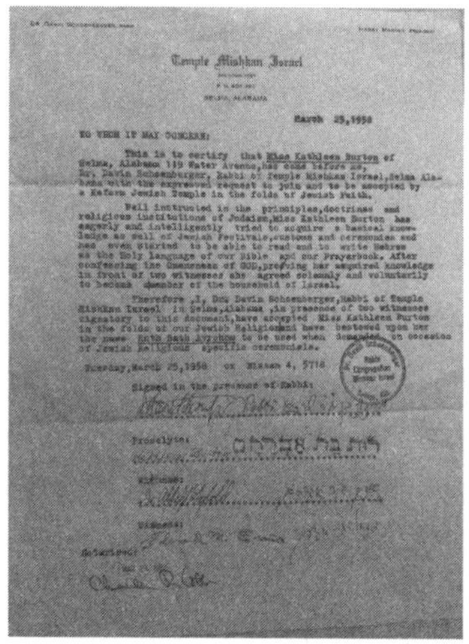

Temple Mishkan Israel

Selma, Alabama

March 25,1958

TO WHOM IT MAY CONCERN:

This is to certify that Miss Kathleen Burton of Selma, Alabama 119 Water Avenue, has come before me, Dr. Devin Schoenberger, Rabbi of Temple Mishkan Israel, Selma Alabama with the expressed request to join and to be accepted by a Reform Jewish Temple in the folds of Jewish Faith.

Well instructed in the principles, doctrines and religious institutions of Judaism, Miss Kathleen Burton has eagerly and intelligently tried to acquire a basical knowledge as well of Jewish Festivals, customs and ceremonies and has even started to be able to read and to write Hebrew as the Holy language of our Bible and our Prayerbook. After confessing the Oneness of GOD, proving her acquired knowledge in front of two witnesses she agreed solemnly and voluntarily to become a member of the household of Israel.

Therefore, I, Dr. Devin Schoenberger, Rabbi of Temple Mishkan Israel in Selma, Alabama, in presence of two witnesses signatory to this document, have accepted Miss Kathleen Burton in the folds of our Jewish Religion and have bestowed upon her the name Ruth Bath Avrohom to be used when demanded on occasion of Jewish Religious specific ceremonials.

Tuesday, March 25, 1958 or Nissan 4, 5718

Signed in the presence of Rabbi:

Proselyte: רות בת אברהם

Witness:

Witness:

Rabbi:

The conversion certificate of Kathleen Burton Weill, the author's mother

I HIRED A PUBLICIST NAMED MOSHE SCHULMAN, COINCIDENTALLY Jewish, to help publicize my memoir *Exhale.*

One November morning in 2020, Moshe and I were discussing our marketing strategy when he suggested that we should submit the book to the Jewish Book Council for consideration for its book awards and inclusion in their newsletter and various book events.

"Great idea, Moshe, but the book's not about anything of interest to a Jewish audience . . . and I'm not Jewish."

Moshe said, "You write about your father who escaped from the Nazis."

I paused. "Oh. That."

"Yes, that," Moshe laughed.

"Your mother is Catholic, right?" Moshe asked.

"Baptist," I said.

"Did she convert to Judaism before she married your father?"

"I don't think so." I thought I would have known if she did, but as I sat there on the phone, I was suddenly unsure. "Does it matter?" I asked.

Moshe laughed again. My naivete about religion generally and Judaism specifically must have struck him as humorous, if not downright odd. "Well, if she did, you're Jewish." Was this some sort of rule I was unaware of?

"I'm Catholic." I stood my ground, imagining myself at the church altar with the priest and the whole flock standing behind me, defiantly in support.

"Technically, not. Even if you converted, in the eyes of the Jewish faith, once Jewish, always Jewish," Moshe said gently, sensing that this might be upsetting to someone like me who had spent a lifetime haunted by the "*What religion are you?*" question until I was baptized at age fifty.

Catholic. I was Catholic, dammit.

I tried to make light. "You mean once you check in, you can't check out?"

"Exactly," Moshe said.

Why is religion so damn complicated? Why couldn't I have just been born into some religion—any religion—and just have gotten on with it?

"Can I call you back?" I asked Moshe. "I need to call my mother."

"Hey, baby," my mother answered the phone with her soft, lilting Southern voice. Usually we would engage in some quick chitchat at the beginning of our daily conversations—books, the weather, politics, my daughters, books—but today I got right down to it.

"Did you convert to Judaism before you and Dad got married?" I asked with some degree of urgency, despite trying to put on my "doctor cool" demeanor.

"Yes."

Yes. I started pacing with the phone plastered to the side of my head.

When? "Right before your father and I were married. I finished the process on March 25, 1958." Six years prior to my birth—to the day. Of course.

Where? "In Selma, at the only synagogue in town." There's a synagogue in Selma, Alabama? I had spent weeks at a time there in the summers when I was a boy and, looking back, thought the likelihood of having a synagogue in Selma—and therefore, I suppose, Jews—was about as likely as both being present on Mars.

What did your parents think of your converting? "They weren't happy about it." *No, I suspect not.*

Finally, I asked, "So why did you convert?"

"The Jewish religion seemed like a sensible one. And the Jewish authors were always so interesting to me." *That was it?*

"Did Dad want you to convert, did his parents?"

"His father thought it was a good idea but, more than that, it just seemed like the right thing to do. We were getting married." So maybe it was a generational thing? The wife takes the husband's religion, even though my father's interest in religion was zero or less than zero. That was what was done. No questions asked.

She told me what she was thinking at the time. There was no more to it. That was it. But I couldn't just drop it. I needed more information—my maybe Jewish/maybe Catholic status was back in doubt, unacceptable but sadly familiar.

So this time, I decided to take action. *Take control of this,* I told myself, so I started a search, an exploration that I hoped would bring understanding, and just as importantly, provide answers to questions that I had posed to myself my entire life.

I did what I do. I read and researched and talked to people who knew about these things. I started writing in longhand in a tattered journal in which I keep many of my ideas, some silly, some not. This was not silly.

It was time to get to the bottom of things.

PART TWO

DISCOVERY

Who looks outside dreams; who looks inside awakes.

—*Carl Jung, Letters, Vol. 1*

Kathleen Burton Weill, the author's mother, circa 1977

CHAPTER ONE

KATHLEEN BURTON WEILL AKA RUTH BATH AVROHOM

New Orleans, 2024

I SAT WITH MY MOTHER IN THE LIVING ROOM OF HER APARTMENT overlooking the Mississippi River. It was late in the afternoon on a sunny day in early April, neither too hot nor too cold, the last bit of bearable weather before the summer's notoriously oppressive heat descended on the city.

My mother and I talked on her couch for a few minutes about common subjects—my kids, Jackie, my sisters—and watched the massive container ships on the river slowly navigate the dark, muddy water. After several minutes, she handed me a plain beige folder containing a document that was only a single page but punched way above its weight in terms of significance to me.

At the top it read: *Temple Mishkan Israel, Founded 1867, Selma, Alabama*. I lingered on the heading for a moment. My mind went back—way back—to the Selma of my youth, bits and pieces of those days flashing before me: my grandparents' modest house on 119 Water Avenue, walking past the neighbors' houses as they waved from their porches, peeling snap beans on the back steps with my grandfather, chasing lightning bugs at night with my sisters. I remembered there was a White section of town and a Black one; I knew where the dividing line was even as a young boy.

And of course, the Edmund Pettus Bridge.

One thing that would seem out of place when I thought of Selma was a synagogue, especially one that had been there since right after the Civil War—or as it was called in the Selma of my youth, the War of Northern Aggression.

The document in my hand certified that Dr. Davin Schoenberger had accepted my mother into "the folds of the Jewish Faith" and that she was "well instructed in the principles, doctrines, and religious institutions of Judaism." I paused, wondering what my grandparents thought of all this. The document went on to say that my mother "eagerly and intelligently tried to acquire a basic knowledge of Jewish Festivals, customs, and ceremonies and has even started to be able to read and to write Hebrew."

I laughed at this last part. "Can you read or write any Hebrew now?" I asked. She looked at me with a shy smile. "No, indeed not. I can't remember much of anything." My mother, like many people her age, said things like this all the time, even though her memory was not nearly as bad as she said it was.

The document then said that my mother was given the name Ruth Bath Avrohom "to be used when demanded on occasion of Jewish religious specific ceremonials." The document was dated March 25, 1958, or the Jewish month of Nissan 4, 5718. My mother's conversion was completed exactly one week before she married my father.

I looked over at my mother, who was watching me as I read. "Well, there it is, I guess," I said, a silly throwaway line I used despite having so many questions. *Why did you convert? If Dad was Jewish and you converted, then why were we raised without religion? Why go to all that trouble if we weren't going to practice Judaism?*

"Tell me how this whole Jewish thing came about?" I asked.

Our family tended to minimize difficult subjects, if they were discussed at all. My mother ran her left palm over her pant leg, periodically bringing her hand up to cover her eyes. At close to ninety, she was getting increasingly light sensitive. Much of the time when I visited, I found her sitting in her apartment in the near dark. Even more than most people, I thought, my mother's eyes were precious to her, to the point of obsession with their health. She often told me if she couldn't read, she would rather be dead, which wasn't hyperbole. I'm always afraid when I hear her say this. When I have suggested audiobooks, she's scoffed at the notion. *I don't know how to work those silly devices.* My mother has a significant luddite streak that sometimes gets in the way of an easier, more connected life.

"I was always interested in Judaism, from the time I first heard about Jews in the church," she said. "God's chosen people. Their role in the Bible, and all the rest. I read the Jewish authors when I was young. Saul Bellow. Bernard Malamud. Norman Mailer. I even dated a Jewish veterinarian in Selma." After a pause, she quickly added, "Before I met your father."

"I was hoping that," I said with a smile.

"They always seemed like such practical people." She said it as a matter of fact. To her it *was* a matter of fact, simple, not worthy of much explanation.

I tried to dig a bit deeper. *What about your religion? Baptism. Why did you turn your back on it?*

My mother paused for a moment, staring out past me, back to when she was young, I thought. "We went to church all the time, during the week, at night, whenever. It was the First Baptist Church of Selma. All our friends were there, all my parents' friends." She smiled. Memories like these made my mother happy, I could tell, but it wasn't clear how often she accessed them. She wasn't one to share her innermost thoughts.

Then the smile left her face. "But it was what the preachers said on Sunday that didn't make sense to me anymore . . . especially as I grew older."

What things, Mom? What things did they say?

She put her hands in her lap, interlocking her fingers. She wasn't afraid to say it, I sensed, but saying it was giving her some degree of pain. "About how we should love All God's Children . . ." She rolled her eyes. "About treating everyone the same . . ." I waited for more—and she gave it to me. "Which obviously wasn't true considering what those same people did the rest of the week. The way they treated the Black folks in our town."

And that was it for you?

"That was it. And what they said about Catholics, too, right from the altar." She shook her head.

I thought back to that time period for a moment, trying to put what she was saying, her reaction, into some kind of historical context. This was the Deep South of the mid- to late 1950s. The Civil Rights Movement had not quite taken hold yet. There was just prejudice and discrimination, plain and simple—and it was all there to see for a young girl from Selma. She would be leaving at the first chance, that much she knew, as she sat in the pews and looked up at the huge rendering of Jesus behind the altar, a flock of children, White children, at His feet.

She would be leaving the church, yes, but also, Selma, to head to New Orleans for nursing school. During this period, New Orleans wasn't thought of as a paragon of racial justice, but compared to Selma it might as well have been a nirvana of harmony and equality.

What did Grandmother and Peck think of all this? Peck was the name my grandfather went by, to his friends and family alike.

"Not much," my mother said, laughing a bit at the question. "But I was gone from their house to my new life, in this city." She gestured toward the sliding glass door that looked out on the Mississippi River.

"And you soon met Dad."

"And I soon met your father."

"The German Jewish immigrant you brought home to Selma," I said, mostly to get a reaction. "That must have gone over well, too," I said, sarcastically.

She shook her head slightly. "No, it didn't. But by that time, I was going to do what I was going to do." In recent years, I have learned so much about my mother, her resolve, her fervent interest in self-determination, her ability to call it as she sees it. She would live where she wanted, how she wanted, and, sometimes I feared, *if* she wanted. I didn't understand these aspects of her when I was younger.

"Well done, Mom. Glad you did."

"Me, too." She tilted her head back, satisfied, it seemed, with the choices she had made.

My mother and I talked further, for over an hour, as the sun began to set over the Mississippi. The bright reflections coming off the water made their way into my mother's apartment and led us both to cover our eyes. Over the course of that afternoon, I found out so much about my mother's family that I didn't know.

The Burton family had come from England more than a century ago and settled in Virginia, where her father, Peck, had grown up. His work with the railroad brought him to Selma, a busy depot at the time. Many of my mother's ancestors fought for the Confederacy in the Civil War. Some had lost their lives, or limbs, others tried to remake their lives in the "New South" after the war.

Toward the end of the conversation, I decided to broach a subject that I knew might be difficult for my mother: her father, my grandfather. Over the years, I had heard bits and pieces about Peck, and I had my own personal experiences with him. When he and I weren't on the back steps peeling snap beans, he would let me hold his rifle. I'd take aim at squirrels in the trees and feel like a real hunter, even though I knew the gun wasn't loaded, or at least I didn't think it was. He gently kidded me when my hair got too long. "Boy, you look like a hippie." I got the impression that this wasn't a compliment, but Peck was always kind to me.

I also suspected there was a darker side to him, a perception that was pieced together with comments my mother made on the rare occasion she would reveal aspects of her childhood to me.

"I would stay in my room when he came home. I could tell by the way he came in the door—just by hearing the door open—if he was drunk or not. Then I could hear him yelling at my mother. That's how I got so into reading. I would use a flashlight under my bedcovers—and stay up all night, to go to another place."

And read the Jewish authors? I said, trying to lighten the mood, pivoting away from memories that must have been seared into my mother's soul, and now mine.

"Sometimes, or the Southern writers. All the usual ones. Faulkner, Harper Lee, Mark Twain, those folks."

What else about him?

"Well, he was good to me. I was his little girl, I guess . . . like your daughters are to you . . ."

I remember he would drop the N-word around the house.

My mother nodded. "Yeah, he did—and worse, I think . . ."

What was worse? I wanted to know.

"He would go off to meetings some nights."

What kind of meetings?

"He called them council meetings, or something like that."

Was that the Klan?

My mother laughed. "You've seen too many movies about the South back then. Not all racists wore white hoods. Most wore suits or work clothes. They were bankers, businessmen, farmers. Just regular folk . . . who hated Black people, that is."

And you grew up around those people?

"Yeah, they were in Selma . . . most of the people there."

And the Black people there?

"I would talk with them, but not much. We weren't friends—they didn't go to school with us, not back then. The first Black people I really interacted with were those I met when I came to New Orleans. And my first real Black friend was Deborah." Deborah worked in our house for many years.

Then her face brightened into a wide smile.

"I remember one time when my mother came to stay with you and your sisters when your father and I went out of town. When we got back home, my mother said, 'And Deborah, she and I ate dinner together one night, just like two people.' She was surprised, I guess, that that was even possible. She had never experienced that before."

My mother was retelling a story I already knew, when I overheard her conversation with my grandmother on the stairs of our childhood home. Just then I pictured my grandmother and Deborah sitting at the kitchen home in our childhood home, quietly eating dinner, perhaps enjoying something Deborah had made, a gumbo or red beans and rice. I imagined that they didn't have much to say to each other, no real understanding of the other's life experience, perhaps only having us children in common, maybe talking about my sisters and me.

In that moment, I felt sorry for both of them, my grandmother and Deborah, for different reasons, but sorrow nonetheless.

As the afternoon turned to evening, it was time for me to go. Jackie had texted me over an hour ago that we were meeting friends for dinner. This was a heavy afternoon, I thought, as I got up and kissed my mother on the top of her head. I would be physically present at dinner but my thoughts would be still in Selma.

Selma, Lord, Selma.

CHAPTER TWO

HANNAH WEILL

Selma, 2022

The Edmund Pettis Bridge, Selma, Alabama, 2022

A FEW MONTHS LATER, I FLEW TO NORTH CAROLINA SO that I could drive home from college with my oldest daughter, Hannah.

As we drove toward New Orleans, leaving the Carolina mountains and then the Atlanta traffic behind us, we chatted about school and Hannah's plans for the summer, and we laughed about finding "common ground" in the music we listened to along the way. In the midst of the trip, as the mind-numbing part of the drive set in, I had an idea.

"We should drive through Selma," I said, one eye on Hannah and the other on the road.

"Where?" she asked.

"Selma. Where Gammie grew up."

Hannah got out her phone and tapped the map function. "It's only thirty minutes or so out of the way. Let's do it," she said, so I pointed the car toward Selma.

After driving for a few hours, we went by the Selma City Limits sign, then passed an empty golf course on the way into town. "119 Water Avenue," I said to Hannah, telling her the address of my mother's childhood home.

We passed through some sites that were vaguely familiar, deeply buried images from over forty years ago that I tried to place. When we drove through the Old Live Oak Cemetery, though, I knew we were getting close. The cemetery was founded in 1829 and was the burial site for several Confederate leaders. I remembered that my sisters and I would hold our breath as we passed through the narrow oak-lined streets that bordered the cemetery. I told Hannah to do the same, and we both held our breath until we burst out laughing at the silliness of it.

We turned a sharp corner onto Water Avenue. The street scene was not what I remembered, not at all. Far from the idyllic lower-middle-class neighborhood of the 1960s and seventies, the neighborhood had a distinctly different feel, and time had not been kind to it. The lawns were poorly kept, the houses in disrepair. There were tattered pieces of furniture in the front lawns of some of the houses. A group of men stood in front of a garbage can that held a small fire, passing a bottle in a brown paper bag. It was ten thirty in the morning.

Then I recognized the house, which was smaller than I remembered it and much more poorly maintained. The screen door in the front had come off one of its hinges and a few kids' bikes were carelessly strewn across the front yard, which had patches of dirt amid brown grass. We pulled up to the curb, and I took a moment to take it all in. Not totally trusting my memory, I took a picture of the house to review later, but also to show my mother, perhaps, when I got home. I'm not sure she would want to see it, but I could decide when I got back to New Orleans if I wanted to show her. Hannah looked out the passenger window for a while, then turned to me.

"Is it how you remembered it?"

"Yes and no. More run down. My grandmother kept a pretty tidy house. She wouldn't be thrilled with the look of the place now."

As we sat there, a Black woman, perhaps in her thirties, opened the front door and stared at us, neither in a menacing nor welcoming way. I figured she didn't get many folks stopping by the house to take a look. Soon, two children, a boy and a girl perhaps around ten or twelve, nudged by her and ran out the door, each picking up one of the bikes in the front. Both sped off down the street. The woman gave us one last look and closed the door.

"Let's go," I said. "I want to make one more stop."

I pulled our rental car into the small parking lot near the Edmund Pettus Bridge. At the base of the bridge stood the National Voting Rights Museum and Institute, which chronicles the events leading up to the 1965 Selma to Montgomery marches and passage of the Voting Rights Act. As the museum describes in its mission statement, it recognizes people, events, and actions that furthered America's Right to Vote since "the Founding Fathers first planted the seeds of democracy in 1776."

Hannah and I went in and walked through the museum's several rooms and exhibit areas that included the "Footprints to Freedom" room, which featured molded cast-footprints of some of the activists who participated in the Selma to Montgomery marches. There was also a "Women's Suffrage Room," honoring the contributions of Black and other women who secured women's voting rights in the United States. We came upon large blow-ups of iconic photographs taken of a Selma to Montgomery march by *Look* magazine photographer James Karales.

Among the 29,500 people who lived in Selma in the 1960s, Blacks outnumbered White people, but the city's voting rolls reflected the electorate as 99 percent White. After a series of racially charged events, the leaders of the Southern Christian Leadership Conference in Selma decided to defuse the community's anger by planning a long march—fifty-four miles—from Selma to the state capitol at Montgomery to draw attention to the violence and voter suppression. As the protesters crossed the Edmund Pettus Bridge—named for a Confederate brigadier general, Grand Dragon of the Alabama Ku Klux Klan, and US senator who stood against basic rights for Black people—state troopers and other law enforcement officers met the unarmed marchers with billy clubs, bullwhips, and tear gas. That was what put Selma on the map—and not in the most flattering light.

My thoughts drifted back to my mother, her beliefs shaped in this town, by these events—and surely passed on to me. After thirty minutes or so in the museum, I said to Hannah, "Let's take a walk."

We slowly ascended the bridge, periodically peering over the side to look at the muddy waters of the Alabama River passing below. The midday traffic was light and slow moving. No one seemed in a hurry in Selma, a small town in the South that was getting smaller each passing year. There was no opportunity there now, not for Blacks, and not for Whites. One got the sense, depressing in many ways, that those who *could* move out of there, generally did. Those that remained had only the bridge as the town's sole attraction.

"The bridge is smaller than I thought it would be," Hannah said when we reached the top. I had a look around, down the other side and back down to the water below. "Yeah, but huge in terms of its significance." Hannah nodded. She knew.

"My mother would bring me here when I was young. Amazing to think that was only around ten years after Bloody Sunday." I thought just then how fresh that must have been, for my mother, her parents, and the whole town—really, for the whole country. "We've made some progress," I said, partly to reassure myself that was true, then qualified it, "at least, in some ways. I guess, not in other ways."

"Did Gammie catch flak from her parents about the whole Civil Rights thing, her involvement?"

"Yeah," I nodded. "My grandparents, her parents, were on the wrong side of things." And then not wanting to sound too judgmental, I said, "A lot of people were. Not just here but everywhere."

We spent a few minutes more snapping pictures and taking in the view. "Okay, ready?" I asked.

"Yep," Hannah replied.

"One more stop," I said.

Hannah laughed. "You said that before we came to the bridge."

"Yeah, but this time I mean it."

We slowly drove away from the Edmund Pettus Bridge down Broad Street. Vibrant would not be the word I would use to describe Selma's main thoroughfare. A few businesses were still there—a coffee shop, a bank, a tired-looking dime store. The Broad Street of the sixties and seventies had nattily dressed people walking up and down, small diners and department stores that, if not luxurious, at least had steady foot traffic.

"There it is," I said to Hannah. I pulled to the curb and pointed at a large red brick building that dwarfed the structures around it.

"What is it?"

I pointed at the Star of David at the top of the building. "A synagogue."

"In Selma?" Hannah asked, appropriately surprised.

"In Selma," I said.

We got out and walked up the front stairs of the red brick structure. I tried the door, but it was locked. We circled the entire building, looking to see if anyone was there. No one. We walked back to the front and spotted a large plaque on a signpost near the street. *Temple Mishkan Israel. Built in 1899, providing a home for the Selma Jewish community that began to organize in the 1830s.* Hannah and I silently read the plaque, which further said: "Members of Mishkan Israel's congregation were vital to the early economic growth of the city. Many of the stores and businesses that lined the streets of downtown Selma were once owned and operated by members of the Jewish community." I supposed the role of the Jewish community in Selma wasn't terribly different from the role of many Jewish communities across the South, and beyond. I later found out that the Temple Mishkan had a Facebook group with thirty members. I joined the group soon after I got back to New Orleans.

"This is where Gammie converted," I said.

"Converted?" Hannah asked. "I thought she was Baptist."

"Was. She converted right before she married my father."

"Oh."

"Yeah, I just recently found out, too."

Hannah quickly put it together. "Wait. So does that make you Jewish? When you became Catholic, you didn't have any formal religion."

"I didn't, but I was Jewish, at least by the 'laws' of the religion. Or so I've come to find out."

"Oh." Hannah thought for a second. "So what does that mean?"

I put my arm around her and smiled. "Still trying to figure that out." I took one last look at the synagogue. "Let's go. Four more hours to go. Better get on the road."

We got back in the car and drove toward New Orleans.

As we left Selma behind in the rearview mirror, I was sure that would be my last visit to my mother's hometown. There was no reason to go back. I knew what I needed to know about the place—and the role it played in my life.

The Kippenheim Synagogue, Kippenheim, Germany, 2025

CHAPTER THREE

THE RABBIS

Kippenheim, Germany, 1360–1939

SITTING IN MY HOME OFFICE DURING THE 2023 THANKSGIVING holiday, soft thunder in the distance, I carefully opened the black leather briefcase and peered inside, a Pandora's box if there ever was one.

The briefcase was well-worn, the gold initials "HW" faded over the many decades since my father bought it. When he died in 2013, my mother gave it to me and said there was some "stuff inside." At the time, in a state of overwhelming grief, I looked only briefly through the contents. I was interested then in what was inside, but not as interested as I am now, ten years later. Time and circumstances had piqued my curiosity, the unanswered questions and blank spaces in my family's past increasingly untenable.

I pulled out a group of documents that were held together by a brown leather binding that had seen better days. The title page read *Ahnentafel Der Kinder Des Nathan Weill in Kippenheim* (or, Ancestral Table of the Children of Nathan Weill in Kippenheim). I opened the tattered pages, being careful not to tear any of them, a real possibility that I wanted to avoid. The document was written in German with tables attached that contained a detailed family tree dating back to the fourteenth century. Fortunately, next to the original, was a bound English translation.

Using a quick internet search, I discovered that the original genealogy was commissioned by Leopold Weill in the early 1930s. Leopold was a wealthy businessman who, incidentally, employed two brothers of the composer Kurt Weill—Natan and Hans—and like most of my ancestors, hailed from the town of Kippenheim or from the area closely surrounding it.

Our family name has taken a few different iterations over the years including Weil, Weyl, and, most recently, Weill. The patriarch of the family was Juda Weil, born in 1360 and likely originally came from Spain. Juda's son, Rabbi Jakob ben Yehuda Weil, was born around 1380 in a small town called Weil-der-Stadt and served as a rabbi in Nuremberg, Augsburg, Bamberg, and Erfurt until his death in 1456. He was a halachic scholar, which involves the study of Talmudic legal matters, and his writings were posthumously published beginning in 1549.

Records are available for rabbinical families for much the same reason that genealogical histories exist for royalty. Rabbis, including those in my family's distant past, were identified with the towns they served, the *yeshivot* (religious academies) they attended or led, and the books they authored. The reason the Weill family could be traced over a six-hundred-year span is because of the numerous writings that were left behind by my ancestors. These written materials were the breadcrumbs left by family, the bits that I was now trying to piece together into some sort of coherent picture.

Jakob's two sons also became rabbis, completing the trio of grandfather-father-son rabbis who formed the foundation of the family. Around 1650, there was a brief interruption of the rabbi lineage when Rabbi David's three sons converted to Christianity despite their intense study of the Talmud, thus establishing a lineage that was Christian while other branches of the family continued on as rabbis. A few family members ultimately went beyond simple conversion to become Christian theologians.

Beginning in the eighteenth century, most of the family settled in the Kippenheim area. At one time, there were well over a thousand Weill family members located there. Smaller Weill groups settled in distant locations including Prague, Ukraine, and the Alsace-Lorraine region of France. After World War II, only fifty Weill family members could be found scattered around the larger German cities: Berlin, Hamburg, Cologne, Frankfurt, Munich, and Vienna. Today, twelve miles south-southwest from Kippenheim is a town called Weill, situated on a plateau called Pleine de Weill, and only a few miles west of Kenzingen is a place called Wyhl.

Selma Stern-Taeubler was another Weill descendant of the same generation as my grandfather Kurt Weill and the composer Kurt Weill. She was an archivist at the American Jewish Archives in Cincinnati and author of the novel *The Spirit Returneth*, published in 1946. The book is a work of historical fiction that portrays the family of Juda Weil, especially the family's eventual tragic experience in the fourteenth century when nearly all Jewish communities along the Rhine River were destroyed, barbarism that foreshadowed what would come centuries later in Hitler's Germany.

* * *

My grandfather Kurt and his cousin Kurt moved to Berlin in between the two world wars, choosing to leave behind their small-town German life for more enticing possibilities. Having developed a close relationship, the two men with the same name were attracted to all the city life that Berlin had to offer—cultural events, entertainment of all kinds, and, from what I have learned, women. It was the Roaring Twenties after all. But the presence in Berlin of my family members, or any Jews for that matter, was fairly recent. Until 1669, Jews had been banned from settling in Berlin or anywhere in the adjacent region. But unlike most other German cities, Berlin did not confine Jews to a ghetto; they were allowed to live anywhere they pleased.

Although small in numbers, in a relatively brief period the German Jewish community produced a staggering array of entrepreneurs, artists, writers, entertainers, scholars, and political activists. This group included Albert Einstein and Karl Marx, whose true home, we now know, was not "Germany" but rather German culture and language. No other class in Germany (or the rest of Europe) carried the love of art to greater lengths than middle- and upper-middle-class Jews in turn-of-the-century Germany.

Much of what is remembered and admired today as the golden age of Weimar culture was created by German Jews, from Einstein's theory of relativity to Magnus Hirschfeld's research on sexuality to Edmund Husserl's philosophy. Kurt Weill's operas could objectively be considered worthy of inclusion among these important German cultural leaders. Between visiting museums and attending Weill's *Threepenny Opera*, tourists flocked to his lectures, charmed by his humor and dazzled by his expansive intellect.

In Berlin between the world wars, the German Jewish influence reached its apex; artists and intellectuals strove as never before to transcend nationality and religion. After the trauma of World War I,

Germany could not have been in more dire need of such an effort. Einstein was perhaps Berlin's most famous "genius." Early members of the press followed Einstein around, falling over one another with their cameras and lights, even photographing the holes in the soles of his shoes. Einstein stuck his tongue out at them—these precursors to the modern-day paparazzi—and called them *Lichtaffen* (flashbulb monkeys). Society ladies flocked to Berlin's golden-domed grand synagogue on the Oranienburgerstrasse to hear Einstein play Bach on the violin.

Religious identity was a significant issue during this period. Some German Jews converted to Christianity on their own initiative and not in response to proselytizers. In fact, most Jews were motivated entirely by pragmatic considerations. Converts came mostly from secularized families and conversion was mostly a middle- and upper-middle-class phenomenon. Before conversion, most converts were non-practicing Jews; after conversion, these former Jews usually became non-practicing Christians.

The richest, most talented, successful, and cultured men and women were often the first to convert. Intermarriage became common, increasing from 8 percent in 1901 to 30 percent in 1915. Fewer and fewer Jews, especially the educated and rich, were observant. The rate of baptisms among Jewish men jumped from 8.4 percent in 1901 to 21 percent in 1918.

Between the world wars, Jews constituted 5 percent of the Berlin population but paid more than 30 percent of the city's taxes. In Hamburg, where the Christian bourgeoisie was said to be far less prejudiced than that in Berlin, half the Jewish population lived in the two wealthiest quarters, Harvestehude and Rotherbaum, and almost half of all private banks were said to be in Jewish hands. The most important among them—the Reichsbank, the Deutsche Bank, the

Dresdner and Darmstädter banks—had been founded, or were still run, by Jewish directors. After the hyperinflation of 1922 wiped out the savings of so many, Germany moved to the right and even the far right, which decried "Jewish capitalism."

Fifty thousand Jews left Germany in 1933, thirty thousand in 1934, and twenty thousand in 1935. Among those who stayed, suicides were rampant. The rest remained, at least for a while, unwilling or unable to leave. Many, including my father's family, refused to believe that the nearly two-thousand-year-old Jewish presence in Germany was coming to an end. Said one prominent Jewish leader: "I am German forever, a German nationalist . . . the Nazis are un-German."

If the situation in Berlin was deteriorating, what was happening in Kippenheim, the center of the Weill family lineage?

I turned to a book by Michael Dobbs called *The Unwanted: America, Auschwitz, and a Village Caught In Between*, a well-researched piece of work that provides important insights into the Kippenheim milieu that many of my ancestors experienced. Dobbs, a former reporter for *The Washington Post* who is now on the staff of the US Holocaust Memorial Museum in Washington, DC, weaves all these elements together seamlessly in an account that lays bare the cruelty and indifference that enveloped German Jews from 1933 onward.

Kippenheim is located in Germany's southwestern Baden region, nestled in the foothills of the picturesque Black Forest. On the eve of World War II, Kippenheim's population was 1,800. Jews arrived in Kippenheim in the seventeenth century and gradually prospered. In 1808, the grand duke of Baden became the first German ruler to offer his Jewish subjects the promise of civil and religious equality if they conformed to German cultural and educational practices. It was an offer the majority of Jews heartily embraced. By then, the Jewish citizens had established successful businesses and built a Moorish-style sandstone synagogue in the center of the village. Some Kippenheim Jews, including family members of mine, began spreading out to the nearby cities of Mannheim and Karlsruhe.

When World War I broke out, Jewish men volunteered to serve in the armed forces. Eight Jewish soldiers from Kippenheim were killed in the course of the hostilities. A memorial honoring their sacrifice was erected in a Jewish cemetery in the adjacent village of Schmieheim.

Prior to Hitler's appointment as chancellor of Germany on January 30, 1933, there had been little open friction between Jews and Christians in Kippenheim. The Jews there had benefited from the relatively liberal atmosphere in Baden, long regarded as one of the more progressive regions of Germany. Although Kippenheimers rarely intermarried, those of different faiths walked to school arm in arm, attended each other's funerals and weddings, and wished each other well on religious holidays. But it took less than six years for relations between the two communities to deteriorate to the point where there was no longer a place for Jews in Kippenheim.

Although only three Kippenheimers cast their ballots for Adolf Hitler's Nazi Party in the 1928 general election, by July 1932, the Nazis had increased their share of Kippenheim vote to 36 percent, but still trailed the Catholic-dominated Centre Party with 42 percent. In order to block the Nazis, many Kippenheim Jews gave their votes to Catholic candidates rather than the more liberal political party they had traditionally supported.

Hitler's eventual appointment as chancellor in 1933 sealed the fate of Kippenheim. The tempo of Nazi persecution of Jews picked up throughout the 1930s and the Nazis in smaller towns like Kippenheim turned out to be even more extreme than the Nazis living in larger cities. The synagogue was vandalized and converted into an agricultural warehouse. Jews were forced to sell their companies to Christians for nominal sums. In 1935, local Nazis passed a resolution denouncing Jewish settlement in Kippenheim and Christian-Jewish fraternization. The resolution described Jews as the "mortal enemy" of the Nazi Party and urged Kippenheimers to "eradicate any foreign elements that pose a threat to German culture."

Clearly, there was no longer a place for Jews in the village. Yet "many Christians maintained good relations with their Jewish neighbors in private, while keeping their distance in public," says Michael Dobbs in *The Unwanted.* Jews in Kippenheim felt the effects of Nazi anti-Semitism keenly. On Kristallnacht, on November 10, 1938, several truckloads of Hitler Youth from the town of Lahr descended on the synagogue and wrecked its interior. The Youth wanted to set fire to the building, but Christian neighbors objected, protesting that adjoining "German property" might be burned.

Even before World War I, Jews had begun migrating away from villages like Kippenheim to cities like Karlsruhe and Mannheim in search of greater economic opportunity. The outward migration continued after the war, causing the Jewish population in Kippenheim to decline to 144 in 1933, when, Hitler came to power, from a high point of 323 just sixty years earlier.

Some Jews managed to escape abroad thanks to United States visas, while others were rounded up and sent to a holding camp in Vichy, France. Still others were transported to the Auschwitz-Birkenau extermination camp in Poland. Jews from Kippenheim, having read the writing on the wall, applied for US visas at the American consulate in Stuttgart. The consul general, Samuel Honaker, was sympathetic to the plight of Jews. By mid-1938, the consulate was approving more than 1,500 visas a month, 90 percent of them to Jews. But the overall refusal rate still exceeded 60 percent. Of the 23,000 people who had applied for visas in the past year, some 14,000 were denied a formal appointment.

Despite widespread American opposition to Jewish immigrants, tens of thousands were allowed in between 1933 and 1945, says Dobbs. The figure he cites is 204,085. "Although the United States could clearly have done more to help victims of Nazi persecution, the number of those admitted was scarcely negligible. The only territory that accepted more Jews than the United States . . . was British-administered Palestine," he writes. German Jews whose visa applications had been rejected or who could not leave Germany found themselves increasingly isolated and in great danger.

By the summer of 1942, mass escape was no longer feasible, Dobbs notes. By his estimation, 25 percent of the internees in Gurs and other French camps died, many from malnutrition and typhus. Others were deported to Auschwitz. "Wealth, education and family ties in the United States all contributed to the ability of Jews to organize their escape," Dobbs writes. All of these factors would help my family get to the United States, as well.

Around 522,000 Jews were living in Germany when Hitler came to power in 1933. Roughly a third were killed in the Holocaust. Thirty-one Kippenheim Jews (out of 144 Jews present in 1933) died as a result of Nazi persecution, a death rate of just over 21 percent. Down the road, in Schmieheim, where the Jewish population was poorer and less well connected, the death rate was over 60 percent.

After Germany's defeat, French forces occupied Kippenheim, and all visible traces of the Nazi era were removed. Starting in 1948, a series of trials of local Nazis took place. The Nazi Party leader in the district, Richard Burk, was cleared of "crimes against humanity." According to Sheldon Kirshner in an article in *The Times of Israel*, Burk "blamed subordinates who had long since died or disappeared. The new West German government permitted Holocaust survivors to file legal claims for property either confiscated by the Nazis or sold under duress at absurdly low prices. . . . These were well-meaning gestures by decent Germans, but the Nazis had achieved their overarching objective of rendering Kippenheim *Judenfrei*."

For my family, the only remaining question would be a simple one: Would the persecution of Jews by the Nazis lead to the end of the six-hundred-year history of the Weill family in Germany? What would they do next? How would the Weills respond?

Given what happened next to my grandfather, the answer to these questions would soon become obvious.

CHAPTER FOUR

KURT WEILL, MY GRANDFATHER

Buchenwald Prisoner #6707, 1938

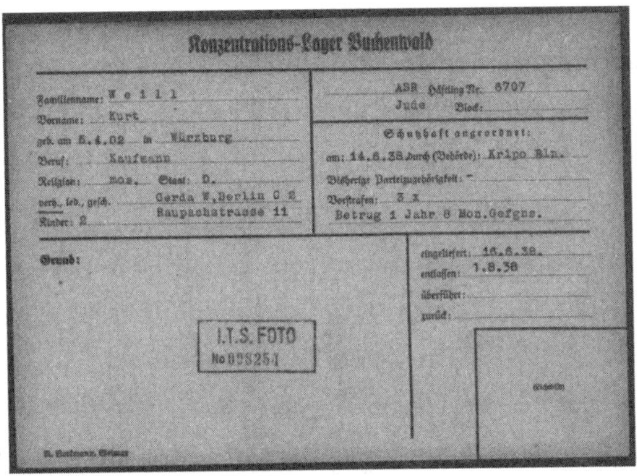

Konzentrations-Lager Buchenwald

Familienname: W e i l l
Vorname: Kurt
geb. am 5.4.02 in Würzburg
Beruf: Kaufmann
Religion: mos. Staat: D.
verh., led., gesch. Gerda W, Berlin C 2
Raupachstrasse 11
Kinder: 2

ASR Häftling Nr. 6707
Jude Block:

Schutzhaft angeordnet:
am: 14.6.38 durch (Behörde): Kripo Bln.
Bisherige Parteizugehörigkeit: -
Vorstrafen: 3 x
Betrug 1 Jahr 8 Mon. Gefgns.

Grund:

eingeliefert: 16.6.38.
entlassen: 1.8.38
überführt:
zurück:

I.T.S. FOTO
No [illegible]

Buchenwald camp records of Kurt Weill, the author's grandfather, 1938

My grandfather, Kurt Weill, was born in Würzburg, Germany on April 5, 1902. After graduating from high school, he entered the workforce as a merchant apprentice. His apprenticeship was interrupted in 1918 when he was drafted into the German Army. After serving in World War I, he worked as a salesman for the Lubitsch company, a furniture wholesaler in Nuremberg. From 1923 to 1928, he had his own business as a tobacco wholesaler.

After moving to Berlin in 1928, Kurt opened a store that sold dry goods such as sheets, pillowcases, and towels.

Kurt's wife Gerda, formerly Gerda Philipp, was born in Berlin on May 26, 1909. After she and Kurt married, Gerda passed her state examination in January of 1928 to become a nursery school and kindergarten teacher at the Pestalozzi School in Berlin-Charlottenburg. Soon thereafter, Gerda ran a preschool out of the family home and had forty to fifty children at any one time.

With an ancestry primarily comprised of rabbinical town leaders, my grandfather chose a different, more secular path. Attracted to the Berlin scene of the 1920s—the Roaring Twenties were in full bloom—Kurt pursued secular interests, including nightlife that naturally attracted a young man in his twenties.

But my grandfather was also searching for his identity in a rapidly changing Germany. In the early to mid-1930s, he was a part-time opinion columnist for a Berlin newspaper, of which there were apparently hundreds at the time. I could find neither the paper he wrote for nor any of his pieces. It was clear though that the world around him was rapidly deteriorating, and my father mentioned to me many times that my grandfather wrote about the changing conditions in Germany—a practice that, my father said, "got him into trouble with the Nazis."

On June 14, 1938, Kurt was taken from his home in Berlin to Buchenwald by the Berlin Criminal Police. My grandfather's arrest card indicated the reason for his arrest: *Weill was repeatedly fined for theft, fraud and embezzlement.* He was sentenced to one year and eight months. The list of items surrendered at the time of his incarceration included a pair of shoes, a pair of socks, a coat, a pair of pants, a vest, one shirt, one pair of underwear, a pair of cuff links, and one mechanical pencil. Given what I was now discovering, and remembering the words from my father, I wonder if something he wrote critical of the Nazis in an opinion piece, aside from, or perhaps in addition to, being Jewish, resulted in his being sent to Buchenwald.

A major source of information about the circumstances that confronted my grandfather after his arrest came from *The Buchenwald Report*. Translated by David A. Hackett, the report was commissioned by the US Army, which sent in a team of German-speaking intelligence officers after Buchenwald was liberated on April 11, 1945. The army team interviewed the prisoners in the hopes of using the information provided in a war crimes case that would ultimately be brought against the Nazis. According to the report, Buchenwald had the distinction of being the first major concentration camp to fall into the hands of the Western Allies while it still had a full population of prisoners. Perhaps because it was the first major camp to be liberated, it received more attention than any other facility.

Buchenwald is located near Weimar in central Germany. Upon liberation, the camp held 21,000 starving prisoners and contained crematoriums, execution rooms, and a hospital used for medical experiments on prisoners. In the spring of 1938, a short time before my grandfather was imprisoned there, the camp housed only about 2,500 prisoners, all of whom were forced into hard labor. The prisoners were engaged in clearing forests; grading roads outside the camp; and building barracks, military quarters, officers' houses, a motor pool garage, and a concrete road to Weimar. They also performed excavations for the laying of cables, worked in a stone quarry, laid water and sewer mains, and built workshops.

In the early months of 1938, the camp was surrounded by an electrically charged barbwire fence. Not infrequently, desperate prisoners chose death by suicide by deliberately running into it. Every day, several prisoners who could no longer bear the torment of being beaten ran through the sentry line and were shot. According to the official designation these prisoners were shot "while attempting to escape."

My grandfather worked daily in the stone quarry, where he and others had to carry stones to the watchtowers around the camp. Aside from this basic fact, the only other information I discovered about my grandfather's time in Buchenwald was gleaned from two letters that he wrote to my grandmother while he was in the camp. The ink had faded over the nearly ninety years since the letters were written—and they were, of course, written in German. I would need to get some help.

I found a German professor at Tulane to translate all the family documents that I had collected.

A reserved woman probably in her forties, Professor Pia Köstner made the short walk from the undergraduate campus to our home on a gray morning in the fall of 2023. This time of day was when I did my best writing, my two labradoodles at my feet, a cup of hot tea on the desk, jazz emanating from my computer speakers, evoking emotions from within me that were hard to conjure up without the music. My mind was usually at its clearest this time of day, my mood generally reflective, my inherent fidgetiness at its most manageable.

But this morning was different. I desperately wanted to know what was written in the German documents that I collected from my sisters and my mother, and the few that I had from my father. I was anxious with anticipation as Professor Köstner rang the doorbell. I greeted her, and we took a seat in my office.

* * *

The previous night, I laid out the documents that I wanted translated, carefully prioritizing them, based on very little except what I vaguely understood them to be. The first set was an easy choice, two handwritten letters from Buchenwald that my grandfather wrote to his wife, the grandmother that I never met. I thought these might provide one of the rare glimpses into my grandfather's mindset as he faced unimaginable circumstances.

I handed Professor Köstner the first letter, a yellowing thin set of pages adorned with fading blue ink on "official" Buchenwald stationery. At the top was my grandfather's name, his camp number 6707, and the date June 17, 1938. He had been at the camp exactly one day, I thought to myself, when the Nazis allowed him to send this letter. But based on what he wrote, he already had the place figured out.

I looked at the professor as she read. At first her expression didn't change—she only periodically pushed her black hair away from her eyes. Then as she turned the pages, she slowly shook her head and then brought her hand to cover her mouth.

What? I wanted to ask.

Finally, after a few more minutes, I did.

"What does it say?" I asked.

"It says, he's healthy and not to worry." I tried to imagine my grandfather writing this, maybe in a bunkroom with rows of prisoners, like the old black-and-white pictures I had seen of the Nazi camps. "He said, to your grandmother, not to be concerned about money." Then she swallowed, this German woman who probably had seen many documents like this before, I suspected. "Send my best to the kids"—my father and his brother—"tell them I'm fine." She paused for a moment. "Then he says his only concern was that everyone—meaning his family, presumably—was healthy." I felt my eyes swelling.

She read for a few more moments. I looked at a picture on my bookshelf of my father and grandfather. My father was a little boy, in his father's arms at the beach in Miami, far away from Germany, Buchenwald, or any place like it. The smile on my grandfather's face was one of pure contentment. He had discovered all that really mattered. He had seen hell and now he knew what heaven looked like.

"I can write a letter twice a month, it says." She read some more. "Then it says at the end: Apply for immigration immediately." This would have gotten by the camp guards who were reading all outgoing mail—at this point, Jewish immigration was being encouraged. The systematic killing would come later. My grandfather was not interested in sticking around to see how it all played out.

I handed the professor the second letter—the same Buchenwald stationery, the same blue ink, the same cautious language. This letter was dated July 3, 1938. "Thank you for the money transfer," the letter started. I tried to imagine what my grandfather might need money for while in the camp, surmising that there was a store of sorts there, a camp canteen with basic supplies. "They allow us to buy Nazi newspapers," the letter said. *Talk about fake news*, I thought.

She read on: "I pray for your health but can't think about you and the kids too much because it's so painful." I pursed my lips, trying to imagine how I would feel, locked up away from my own wife and kids, my fate uncertain. I had trouble getting there in my own mind.

Then to the practical: "Glad there are no money worries. Close the business and pay anyone we owe money to." These were matters, I supposed, that had to be taken care of. Life goes on, after all, until it doesn't.

And then finally, at the end, "Try to move the immigration process along, preferably to the United States." Easier said than done, I'm sure, but the plan was set, my grandfather's intention clear.

* * *

After translating several more documents—the arrest records, a reparations form that was filed by my grandfather in 1957, a few letters back and forth between relatives—the professor got up to leave. At the door, she gently touched my shoulder and said: "You should write this book. It's important."

A heaviness overwhelmed me, then a jolt of determination came from my core and hit my brain like an adrenaline shot. "I'm going to. It won't be easy, but I'm going to."

She nodded. "Your family's been through worse. You can do it." Such a German thing to say, I thought, but a comment that was hard to disagree with. This woman I had just met seemed to understand. She knew the score.

Your family's been through worse. That simple statement could easily be our motto, displayed on a family crest, a coffee cup, or tombstone, displacing *Never complain, never explain* once and for all. From then on, at least as it pertained to my life, that phrase—*Your family's been through worse*—would be my governing philosophy, a guiding principle that I would fall back upon, again and again.

According to documents from Buchenwald, my grandfather was released (*entlassen*) around August 10, 1938. The actual release date is unclear, though it presumably occurred the week prior to the tenth.

My grandfather came out of Buchenwald weighing less than ninety pounds. A small man at five foot four, he was not only emaciated but also ill with a serious lung condition. He contracted silicosis while in the camp as a result of inhaling fractured stone particles while working in the stone quarry. One of the complications of silicosis, and a common communicable disease in all the Nazi concentration camps, tuberculosis exacerbated my grandfather's lung disease, an infection that was of course ignored by his captors. One interesting side note is that my father, who was a prominent pulmonologist, eventually became one of the world's leading experts on silicosis, authoring hundreds of research papers and book chapters on the subject. My grandfather's lung condition and my father's interest in the disease was a connection that I had not previously understood—until now. It was simply something my father never mentioned to me, despite the fact that I too became a pulmonologist, a career choice that was not coincidental, but instead reflected a strong desire to follow in my father's footsteps—to have not only a career in common, but more precisely, a passion in common.

In his weakened condition after he left Buchenwald, my grandfather knew one thing for sure, communicated clearly to his wife over long talks late at night while seated at the kitchen table. My father overheard these conversations as a young boy when he should have been asleep: The family needed to leave Germany as soon as possible because, in my grandfather's words, "they are going to kill us all." His survival instinct had become fine-tuned while inside the gates of Buchenwald.

My grandfather's preferred destination was the United States, but that typically involved a multiyear wait for an immigration visa. Faced with this dilemma and like many family patriarchs, my grandfather faced a set of central questions: Should the family stick together in all circumstances? Should they split up? Or would it be preferable for one of them to emigrate if the opportunity arose?

* * *

On August 30, 1938, the SS *Ile de France* set sail from Le Havre, France and arrived at the port of New York on September 5, 1938. According to the ship manifest, my grandfather was on that boat by himself, his wife and two sons left behind.

> Key information—Line 12: Kurt Weill; 36 years old; male; married; worker; reads and writes German; German nationality; Hebrew race/people; born in Wurzburg, Germany; QIV visa no. 595 issued in Berlin August 27, 1938; Last residence: Berlin, Germany; Left behind in last residence: Gerda Weill at Raupachstr 11 Berlin C2; Destination: New York, NY; Arrival Contact: Brother, Walter Weill at 610 W 152 St, Apt 31, New York, NY

When my grandfather arrived in New York, he had ten Deutschemark in his pocket. He applied for United States citizenship on December 5, 1938.

My father told me that my grandfather left the family behind in order to establish himself in America, to find a place to live and to secure employment. My father also said how difficult it was to see his father leave, especially given the circumstances in Germany in late 1938. He wasn't prone to hyperbole or to emotional reflection, but he said, as a young boy, "he was scared beyond belief" and lay awake many nights waiting for a knock on the door, just as had occurred when his father was arrested and taken to Buchenwald. My own assessment is that that period had a permanent impact on my father, resulting in his emotional distance and an outlook that often seemed to be perpetually waiting for something bad to happen. How could it not?

But my grandfather did what he had to do. As Walter Laqueur, a German-born historian and Holocaust survivor said, "The pessimists left, the optimists died."

When my grandfather moved to Berlin, the Jewish population was 160,000. By the time my father came to the United States in 1939, the number of Jews had been halved to 80,000. Beginning in 1933, the German government revoked German citizenship for tens of thousands of German Jews as well as people seen as political opponents, such as communists.

According to documents from the Ministry of Foreign Affairs Political Archive and Historical Service in Berlin on April 16, 1940, the following was said about my grandfather's German citizenship:

> Subject: Deprivation of the German citizenship of the Jew Kurt Weill, born April 5, 1902 in Wurzburg. I am enclosing two copies of an expatriation application that was forwarded to Department I of the Reich Ministry of the Interior today.
>
> Subject: Application for deprivation of German citizenship; Decree of 12/4/1937; II B3- General 342 E; I am applying for the merchant's German citizenship to be revoked; Weill, Kurt, born 5 April in Wurzburg; Ethnicity: Jew; Last Residence: Berlin, Raupachstr. 11 (Raupach Street); Current residence: New York; Time of emigration: August 27, 1938

My grandfather was officially stripped of his German citizenship a year after he immigrated to America. This was despite having served honorably in the German Army in World War I.

When Kurt made it to New York, one of the Jewish aid organizations got him a job driving a wealthy New Yorker from New York to Miami in September of 1938. The only problem was an important one: He had never driven a car. Not once. But somehow he made it to Miami with only one minor mishap when he tore a sideview mirror off the car while backing out of the gentleman's driveway in New York. But once Kurt made it to Miami, and had one look at the beaches and felt the warm weather, he had found his American home.

Next, he had to get his family out of Germany, something that was not easy to do. The United States was allowing only a limited number of German immigrants into the country during that time period. By combining the German and Austrian quotas, approximately 27,370 predominantly Jewish refugees were allowed to enter the United States every year from German-speaking countries. When my grandmother told friends that she needed to "get away" after my grandfather left Germany, she did not mean out of the house, or even out of Berlin. She meant out of Germany. At the same time in Berlin, tens of thousands of Jews began to hide, squeezing into cupboards in attics and basements, or cowering under beds and bathtubs. Any doubts about what German Jews should do vanished. A single hope remained: emigration.

President Roosevelt was acutely aware of the American anti-immigrant sentiment. In fact, four out of five Americans were opposed to European Jewish immigration of any kind. Perhaps in attempt at rationalizing this disturbing stance, four out of ten Americans informed pollsters that "Jews have too much power in the

United States." Reflecting the sentiment at the time, a spokesman for the anti-immigration forces, Senator Robert Reynolds of North Carolina, denounced the child refugee initiative in a nationwide broadcast.

Our Citizens First.
Let's keep America for our boys and girls.
Let's give American jobs to American citizens.
Let's empty our prisons of alien criminals and send them back to their native lands.
Let's save America for Americans.

If this sort of rhetoric sounds familiar, there is good reason: Many of the same words are used today in certain segments of the current United States political arena.

Giving the US government (and its citizens) the benefit of the doubt, perhaps it was difficult for most Americans, FDR included, to conceive of evil on such a scale. But nonetheless, both the president and Congress had failed the test of leadership. Sensing a void in commitment to the plight of the German Jews, it was left to Nazi officials to comment on the gap between American ideals—as represented by the welcoming arms of the Statue of Liberty—and the reality. "We say openly that we do not want the Jews while the democracies keep on claiming that they are willing to receive them—and then leave the guests out in the cold!" wrote one columnist in the anti-Semitic journal *Der Welkampf.* "Aren't we savages better men after all?"

My father's family found a way to unite once again. According to the ship manifest:

> The S. S. Queen Mary set sail from Southampton, England on February 4, 1939 and arrived at the port of New York on

> February 9, 1939. Gerda Weill is on line 16 and her sons are on lines 17 and 18. They are going to join Kurt Weill at 223 Meridian Ave in Miami, Florida.

In Miami, my grandfather found work in the restaurant business, first busing tables, then as a waiter. By working sixteen-hour days, seven days a week, he eventually saved enough money to open a deli in Miami Beach. When she joined my grandfather in Miami, my grandmother Gerda worked with him, as did my father even while still in elementary school. The deli was near the beach and was accessed through a garage door that, when opened, had a direct view of the Atlantic Ocean, a sight that my father said reminded him each time he looked out at the water of what was happening on the other side of the Atlantic.

My father spent his boyhood years playing on the beach, eventually becoming a lifeguard during the summers. Even at his young age during World War II, my father closely followed the war, devouring the local newspaper each morning to track the Allies' progress. As much as he understood what was at stake—how could he not?—he still explained to me years later how difficult it was to hope for Germany's loss, the country of his birth and whose language was still spoken in the family home.

After he opened his own deli, my grandfather also worked nights in the Balmoral Hotel dining room, eventually ascending to a night manager role—a job associated with more pay, but one that took him away from his family most nights. But as much joy as my grandfather and grandmother had building a life in their new country, all was not well. According to reparation documents, my grandmother was struggling, apparently with mental health issues, an understandable consequence of her experience in the years just prior to her immigration to the US.

According to one of the reparation forms completed by my grandfather: "Since my wife did not feel well after emigration, she was unable to continue her work here. During my imprisonment she suffered a nervous breakdown which she never got over. So not only did she lose her profession because of the Nazi regime, she also lost her health."

In many ways, my father's family led the quintessential immigrant life in South Florida, characterized by hardworking parents, two boys who excelled academically, and, most importantly, a special brand of patriotism that many immigrants feel, especially ones who experience inhumane treatment in their home country. In terms of their religious practice, my father's family did not regularly attend synagogue, but both my father and uncle were bar mitzvahed. My grandfather was indifferent to whether the boys did or did not practice Judaism and, in fact, thought his young family was "too busy" for a formal religious practice. But my grandmother certainly wanted her sons to be bar mitzvahed, so they were. My grandfather was more content with his young family simple being "culturally Jewish" rather than practicing Jews.

Most of the time, cultural Judaism was more than enough to feel assimilated, especially given the number of Jews who had settled in South Florida. One of the few times that my father's Jewishness or his being German came up at all was when Gerda became offended after an elementary school teacher asked if his name could be changed, because the name Hans sounded "too Jewish" and "too German." My grandmother would not hear of it, marching into the school and informing the teacher that she had "picked out my eldest son's name for a reason and wasn't about to change it," according to my father's recollection of these events. Needless to say, my father carried the name Hans to his grave. But when I asked him as a young boy why he didn't name me Hans, since so many of my friends were named after their father, he simply replied with a shrug: "I wouldn't do that to you." That was all the explanation that I got—and I accepted it, even if I didn't understand what he meant at the time.

Kurt and Gerda became official United States citizens on November 13, 1944. All was going well until Gerda noticed having difficulty swallowing one day at lunch. Resistant to seeing a doctor at first, she was eventually told she had esophageal cancer, a devastating diagnosis, then and now. Hans returned home from college to be with her as she received medical treatment.

Sitting every day at her bedside when her end was near, my father was away from his pre-medical studies for a whole semester. He returned to New Orleans after her death in 1952 to complete his freshman year at Tulane, once he was sure his father and brother had recovered from the devastating loss of their wife and mother. In my conversations with my father about his mother, I am not sure he ever allowed himself to fully experience the grief he felt, resulting in a lifelong emotional detachment, often from those he loved the most.

Kurt would eventually die in July 1977. He never remarried or had any love interest other than Gerda. My grandfather's life was a hard one, filled with pain and loss, hard work and struggle, but no one ever heard a complaint from him, and he never wanted anyone to feel sorry for him. The respect I hold for him, especially given all that I have recently learned about his life, is immeasurable. He's a hero to me—so I paid one last visit to him in the only place that I now could.

Mount Nebo Miami Memorial Gardens was established in the 1950s and is the oldest Jewish cemetery in South Florida. According to its website, Mount Nebo is the final resting spot for many "prominent members of the Miami Beach Jewish community."

Situated on thirty acres of land, the Memorial Gardens is just a few miles away from Miami International Airport, making it easily accessible after my short flight from New Orleans in the early summer of 2023.

After landing, I rented a car and drove straight over. When I arrived, it immediately struck me how the cemetery got its name—the grounds were really more like a garden than a burial site, more park than cemetery, with a well-manicured mix of oaks, black olive trees, and palms. I didn't know this before my visit, but I was told by one of the staff there that, in keeping with Jewish tradition, there are no flowers planted in the cemetery. As I walked to my grandparents' grave site, I made a mental note to check why that is the tradition, just another one of the mysteries of the Jewish faith.

My grandparents' tombstones are simply adorned—their names and their dates of birth and death. I stood alone in this whole section of the cemetery and took in the flat ground with rows and rows of plot markers, a few that looked like my grandparents' and some more elaborate. Then I thought: *Elaborate would not be Gerda and Kurt's way, not after what they experienced, not after what I had learned over these many months*. Their plain granite marker just as easily could have simply said, *Never complain and never explain.*

I stood there for around fifteen minutes and then slowly took a knee. I didn't pray, not really. I meditated, on their life, on the lives that came before theirs—and on mine.

Never complain, never explain. I was beginning to understand what this phrase really meant—but there was more.

The composer Kurt Weill, Germany, circa 1920

CHAPTER FIVE

KURT WEILL, THE COMPOSER

Germany, New York, Los Angeles, 1900–1950

THERE WERE CERTAIN THINGS I COULD LEARN ABOUT MY famous relative from reading books about him or from the documents I uncovered in my research, but the essence of the man was something I was missing. The larger question, while hunting for details about various aspects of his life, was: *Who, or what, was Kurt Weill to me, other than a person who made my routinely mispronounced last name recognizable to certain people—primarily those who lived on either American coast, were Jews, or both?*

But perhaps there was an even more important question: *What role, if any, did he have in helping to get my father's family to America?*

New York 2023

I looked at the map app on my iPhone, making sure I was in the right place—the Kurt Weill Foundation. A clear but cold winter morning,

I decided to walk the thirty blocks from my hotel to where I now stood. Thirty minutes later, I arrived at the building on East 20th Street—a narrow, vertical, nondescript, multistory structure above a kitchen and bath fixture store in a part of New York that I had never been.

A few weeks prior, I had left a voice message for the executive director of the Kurt Weill Foundation, Dave Stein. When he called me back, Dave joked that once he heard my last name, he figured I wanted to know what the fuss was about regarding my famous relative. After exchanging a few pleasantries—where I lived, how I was related to Kurt Weill, what my book project was about—Dave asked me, "Are you interested in his music?"

"Ummm . . . well," I stammered, then decided to get right to the point. "Not really." I hesitated, given that the man on the other end of the line had devoted his professional life to the man's music.

"Oh . . ." Dave paused, waiting for me to explain. So I did.

"I want to know more about *him*, his role in my family's story. But really, about *him*. What was he like? And one important question: Did he save my family from the Nazis? Is he the reason my family made it out, why they were allowed into America?" I paused for a beat. "Is he the reason I'm here?"

"I see," Dave said. "Not typically what we hear. But come by the Foundation. We can talk, and I can show you some things."

I hung up and booked a flight to New York.

I sat in the conference room while Dave finished a call. It was not the kind of meeting room with which I'm most familiar—the ones with football field–length tables and high-backed leather chairs. Instead, the room looked more like a middle school library with outdated, simple wooden furniture and musty bookcases adorning each of the four walls.

After a few minutes, I got up and looked at the dusty books on the shelf as I waited, running my hands over the hundreds of volumes dedicated to the man and his music—books about Kurt Weill's formative years; his music sheets; and pictures of him at the piano, cigarette in hand, and dining at a restaurant with a young actress. I picked up one of the first volumes I saw, one adorned with a photograph of the artist as a young man, bespectacled and staring straight into the camera. I pulled the book closer to my face, studying the black-and-white image on the cover.

Did I see me in him? My father? Any of us? I thought I did, the nose, the mouth, the dark hair and eyes. I wondered what he was like. *What was he like?*

My thoughts were interrupted when a tall, thin man with a gray beard and hair pulled back in a ponytail stood before me. "Dave Stein, nice to meet you." We shook hands and I took him in for a moment. He didn't look anything like I expected. I'm not sure what I expected but not this. He looked too young, too hip to be a Kurt Weill aficionado. I guess I had been imagining someone older, more conventional, stodgy even. But Dave looked like he could be the executive director of the Grateful Dead Foundation, not the Kurt Weill Foundation. I moved past my stereotype musings and got down to what I was there for.

"As I said on the phone, I'm working on a book project about my family and my own religious identity. I think Kurt Weill might have been significant to our story, helped my father's family get to the United States."

Dave nodded. "So not the music?"

I thought back to my childhood for a moment, when the obligatory monthly Kurt Weill record was played in our family living room, the listening sessions that my father periodically enforced and my sisters and I unwillingly endured.

"No, not the music. That's not what I'm interested in." Then remembering that I was likely offending the man. "I mean . . . his music is, um, interesting but not my focus." *Not a bad recovery,* I thought.

Dave looked at me for a moment, then away and back to me. "Yeah, I get it. But, if I can make a suggestion?"

"Sure."

"If you want to know something about Kurt Weill, about what made him tick, or how he fit into your family's story, you might want to learn something about his music." Dave said all this in a completely inoffensive way, making the point that to understand an artist, perhaps one should start with their art, which seemed suddenly like an obvious position to take.

I considered his point. *His music,* I thought. Then thought again. *His music.* Yeah, I better know at least something about what he was trying to say with his music.

"You're right. Of course," I said. "Where do we start?"

For the next twenty minutes or so, Dave led me through the bookcases, pulling down one book at a time, stacking them in my arms until I couldn't carry any more.

Finally, sinking under the weight, I said, "Let me start with these—should keep me busy for a while." I put the books down on a table and had a seat. Dave walked back to his office. I looked at the books and ran my eyes down the stack. While I did this, I pulled up a collection of Kurt Weill's music on Spotify, put in my earbuds, and began to listen. I was immediately transported to the living room of my youth, which was nice, even if the music didn't appeal to me.

I took the first book off the top and began to read.

The Artist as a Young Man

Albert Weill was born in 1867 in Kippenheim and married Emma Ackermann in 1897. The couple had four children in successive years: Nathan, born in 1898, became a doctor; Hans Jakob, born in 1899, went into the metal business; and Ruth, born in 1901, became a schoolteacher. Kurt was born in 1900.

Albert was appointed as cantor of the synagogue at Eichstätt in Bavaria when he was in his early twenties. At the turn of the century, the time when Albert took up his new cantor post in Dessau, the city had a Jewish population of around five hundred. The Jews had first been admitted to the town in 1672 and, in 1687, the Jewish community received permission to build a synagogue and establish their own cemetery. The Age of Enlightenment brought Jews and Gentiles closer together through a common pursuit of intellectual growth and humanistic values. However, it was not until 1848, the year of European revolutions, that the Jews of Dessau received their full political, social, and educational rights as "emancipated" citizens.

Whenever he heard his father sing, Kurt was reminded what a strong, beautiful voice he possessed. He was always transfixed when his father sang the familiar Jewish music, and was glad his father had chosen to be a cantor instead of becoming a rabbi, given that Kurt thought music much more interesting than rabbinical pursuits. Even at a young age, Kurt knew that many members of the Weill family had been prominent rabbis and synagogue cantors in this part of Germany as far back as the 1300s and that their writings and compositions had left a mark on the region's Jewish community. But most of all, Kurt loved the fact that music was in the family's blood.

Shortly after the inauguration of the new Dessau synagogue in 1908, Albert Weill and his family moved into the ground-floor apartment provided for the cantor in the Jewish community center that adjoined the synagogue. For all the musical powers at work within him, Kurt had no pretensions of behaving differently from any other normal boy of his age, and took no interest in the adult conversation going on around him. But there was no secret about what mattered most to him. As Nathan said, looking back at their childhood, "Kurt lived only for music." As Kurt worked his way through school, doing just enough to move up from one class to the next at the end of the year, he found the focus of his musical interests changing from the religious to the secular, from the synagogue to the theater.

The Artist in Berlin

By the time he graduated from Oberrealschule (secondary school) in Dessau in March 1918, Kurt had decided to seek further education elsewhere. With the help of Albert Bing, an early mentor, he was able to convince his father that he should add medicine to his music studies, and that both interests could be pursued in only one place: Berlin. My grandfather Kurt was born in Würzburg, and in addition to visiting each other as children, the two of them became even closer when both moved to Berlin as young adults. Sharing an interest in all the cosmopolitan attributes of their new city, the two became more like brothers than cousins.

After having narrowly escaped military service in World War I, Kurt lived through the post-war inflation nightmare in Berlin but was able to ride the swelling wave of cultural excitement through the decade of the Weimar Republic.

Eighteen-year-old future composer Kurt Weill arrived in the German capital at a time of great turmoil—the brutal war still had six months to go. Among its citizens, Berlin was replete with contradictions of all sorts: those who, with a fair amount of defiance, looked backward to more promising times, juxtaposed against the more revolutionary-minded, who were determined to press an effort toward modernization. "Berlin was not just a city, it was a way of life—a larger-than-life way of life. The sky was the limit. But there was a long way to fall," Kurt said.

Looking back, Kurt also said: "After the defeat of Germany we young musicians too were filled with new ideals, aflame with new hopes. But we were not capable of giving shape to the new values which we so earnestly sought, or of finding the proper form for our content. We snapped the chains that bound us but did not know what to do with the freedom we had won. We broke new ground but forgot to glance back. So as a result of being cut off from the outside world for so long we suffered from paroxysms of emotional intemperance which descended on us like nightmares but which we nonetheless held so dear because they had brought us liberation."

Berlin, one of the world's three major capitals, was on its way to becoming a musical and literary paradise. After World War I, there was a rebirth of cultural events. Eighty theaters existed in the city, along with over two hundred movie theaters and three opera houses. Although the country was in a period of severe economic depression, the government offered subsidies to people so they could attend concerts and operas, if they needed financial help.

Berlin's enormous growth in the arts and sciences lasted throughout the 1920s into the mid-thirties, but it also continued to be a city of many social contrasts and during that same time a decadent underbelly developed in the city. Crime, prostitution, and erotic entertainment flourished. Under the monarchy, Berlin had been the repressed, uninspired capital of Prussia; now, new music, literature, theater, and the visual arts found an accepting audience. But there was something else: Its citizens called it *Berliner Luft* (*Berlin Air*) because, along with the arts, the city had an air of openness for sexual matters, manifested by theaters and cabarets, which provided artistic outlets for both straight and gay-themed productions.

In April of 1918, Kurt registered at the Hochschule für Musik in Berlin and began learning about modern composers. At the same time, he took courses in philosophy at the Friedrich Wilhelm University where his teachers included some of Germany's finest minds. Three months later, after receiving the consent of his parents, Kurt dropped all his medical courses and concentrated on musical studies and philosophy. He even became a magazine writer, with a weekly column about German music culture.

Kurt grew up playing organ in the synagogue where his father was the cantor, and he remained active in Jewish life, working at the Jewish Community Center in Berlin.

Still he felt his Jewish heritage restricted his compositional abilities, writing to his brother in 1919 that "We Jews are just not productive, and if we are, then we have a subversive, not a constructive, impact." By 1924, he wrote to his mother that he felt alienated from the Jewish community, and that Jews "are impossible in every way." Still, he continued: "We must find our way back to our childhood faith."

As the direction of Nazi Germany became obvious, certain segments of the German population began to speak of *Amerikanismus*, a term that denoted hope for the political modernity and economic efficiency that America embodied, as well as Germany's entry into a broader international political, economic, and artistic community. To the Germans during this period, America signified cultural youthfulness, unburdened by the centuries of a tumultuous and bloody history that seemed to weigh down Europe.

I looked at my watch. It was 11:30 a.m. and I hadn't moved for two hours, which was quite unlike me. I decided to forge ahead, knowing that I was getting to the good stuff, especially the personal life of the composer and what I wanted to know most: *Who was Kurt Weill, the man?*

Then, I learned a bit more.

Kurt, usually masked behind a placid exterior, was an intense man with a relentless passion to create meaningful art. In the early years of their marriage, his wife, Lotte Lenya, complained of feeling in no way like a newlywed—especially disappointed by a scant sex life—and her patience with him was exhausted. She complained, "What kind of life is this for a married couple?" Kurt, in a famous statement that Lotte frequently repeated even many years later, supposedly answered, "What do you mean, darling? You know you come right after my music!" Lenya very likely knew this to be true, if difficult to accept.

"There are two types of happiness," he told Lotte, "there is a rapture for two, where one is more in one's partner than in oneself; and there is the blissful loneliness of creation, as one gazes silently upon life and mankind. You consider that I turn my back on what is unpleasant. I don't—I drink my fill of it, because it is part and parcel of the age into which I have been born and because it points the way to beauty, which blossoms today as it has always done . . . I savour every emotion to the full, without wondering what it might lead to."

* * *

I smiled as I read this passage. *Sounds a lot like me,* I thought. Maybe I did have things in common with this guy, maybe I did "inherit" his inner life, his relationship to his work and to those around him, to his religion. Perhaps there was a connection—not a direct line but rather a dotted one—between this man and me, one that was never apparent until recently, one that I didn't seek out until now.

I kept reading.

On one matter, the couple was in absolute agreement. As the Nazis rose to power and their intentions became clear, Kurt and Lotte realized there was no future for them in Germany.

Despite his success, Kurt had to leave Germany, and he ultimately decided to move to Paris, arriving on March 23, 1933, "penniless and bedraggled." He established a base in Louveciennes (a suburb of Paris) for the remainder of 1933 and all of 1934, although he traveled extensively, visiting his parents in Czechoslovakia and vacationing in Italy.

Even though Kurt enjoyed the vibrant intellectual and arts scene in Paris, his ultimate goal was to settle in America. He and Lotte had divorced, then reconciled before the couple decided to immigrate to the United States. The Germany of his youth was gone and, for both personal and professional reasons, the United States offered him the most opportunity. On September 4, 1935, Kurt and Lotte boarded the SS *Majestic* in Cherbourg, France, and arrived in New York six days later.

To Lotte's delight, the couple settled in style at the St. Moritz Hotel facing Central Park South. In January 1937, Kurt and Lotte stood before a justice of the peace in Westchester County, New York, and for the second time became Mr. and Mrs. Kurt Weill.

Kurt's parents left Germany in 1935 to go to Palestine. The composer tried to bring his parents to the United States in the early 1940s from Palestine as the Nazis swept through Northern Africa, but this never materialized for reasons that are unclear.

Although Weill applied for citizenship in 1937, he did not complete the process until August 1943. Once the United States entered the war in late 1941, Weill's position as a German immigrant became even more precarious.

The Artist in America

I next opened a book by Naomi Graber called *Kurt Weill's America*, which I hoped would give me insight about what Kurt thought of his new country—and it did.

Kurt was never merely a happily assimilated immigrant. After his arrival, he set to work using musical theater to correct the injustices he observed, even as he declared (and most likely felt) ardent patriotism. In 1944, nine years after he arrived in the United States, Kurt told *New Yorker* magazine, "In every age and part of the world there is a place about which fantasies are written." He continued: "In Mozart's time it was Turkey. For Shakespeare it was Italy. For us in Germany, it was always America."

Like many European immigrants of the 1930s, Kurt hoped to find work in the film industry in California and was well paid for his early efforts on the West Coast, even if many of his creations were left on the cutting room floor. New York seemed to be a better fit for him, both professionally and aesthetically, so he eventually moved back there, finding residence in the same apartment building as Ira Gershwin. Kurt and Ira struck up a friendship, and apparently, the two composers spent many nights together, drinking and smoking while having animated discussions about music.

Starting to get a better sense of the man, his art, his struggles, his relationship to his old and new country, I turned to another book titled *Thousands of Miles: The Life and Musical Journey of Kurt Weill* by Ellen Norman Stern and found an interesting passage written by the American composer and critic Virgil Thomson:

> It has long been the opinion of this reviewer that Kurt Weill's contributions to German theatre were more original than anything he wrote here [i.e. in America]. His American work was viable but not striking, thoroughly competent but essentially conformist. His German works, on the other hand, made musical history.

I thought then how, contrary to what I might have previously believed, Kurt Weill's work was significantly impacted—perhaps not in a positive way—by his immigration to the United States. True, he survived the Nazi period—at least he remained alive—but perhaps other parts of him, especially his main passion in life, didn't fare as well.

The Artist in My Dream

After a long day spent reading about the composer at the Kurt Weill Foundation, I was having trouble getting to sleep in my New York hotel. It could have been the travel, the time zone changes, or something bothering me, causing my mind to be unsettled, an increasingly common state of affairs for me.

Tossing and turning with the lights off, I finally drifted off to sleep—but, despite my intentions to the contrary, I was not quite done for the day with Kurt Weill.

Me: You're supposed to be a big deal . . .

Kurt nodded, agreeing with the obvious.

Me: . . . but the only people that have heard of you have a Manhattan area code . . .

Kurt: Area code?

Me: Live in New York, I mean . . .

Kurt took a drag from his cigarette. I scrunched up my face, then handed him an ashtray that I produced from . . . where?

Me: I grew up in New Orleans. My father didn't seem to know much about you. My only exposure to you was during the occasional times when my father played your music, which to a young boy was pretty awful.

I smiled, trying to soften my words. He remained expressionless.

Kurt: My music was dark, haunting, reflecting a time and place in Germany. Then, the ravages of war . . . You might have heard of the world wars, even in New Orleans . . .

Me: Funny. Yes, we had. You may have recalled that my father's family fled Nazi Germany. His father, your friend and cousin, was in Buchenwald, which nearly killed him.

Kurt: Yes, I recall all that. I saw your grandfather, many times, in New York and visited him in Miami.

He blew a ring of smoke toward the ceiling.

Kurt: And you probably have figured out by now, I was your family's American sponsor. I had to vouch for them so they could get into the United States. But you know that now . . .

Me: Well, then some thanks are in order.

But back to your music. It is . . . um . . . interesting. I've tried, I really have.

Kurt: Well, it's nuanced. Perhaps not for everyone.

He took another drag from his cigarette and, this time, blew out the smoke not up toward the ceiling, but right at me.

Me: I searched Spotify. I found English versions, German versions. "Mack the Knife." Catchy, especially the Bobby Darin version. Oh and "September Song" but not the Doors version, the Sarah Vaughan one.

Kurt: I have no idea what you're talking about.

Me: I also found someone, or something, called Kurt Vile. A punk band, it seems.

Kurt: Punk?

Me: Never mind. Anyway, thanks for getting my family, us, out of Germany.

I reached out my hand and the composer slowly took it in his.

Kurt: You're welcome. Can I say one more thing?

Me: Sure, at this point, why not?

The first hint of a smile from him during this "conversation."

Kurt pointed at his heart.

Kurt: The answer is here. It's all here, not here . . .
He pointed to his head.
Kurt: You're still learning that . . .

The dream ended and I woke, shaken by the dream sequence that seemed so real.

I was done for the night. Sleep would not be coming, after that, after all this. I went to the hotel room desk to go back to work. There was more I needed to know.

Kurt Weill: His Role in My Family's Destiny

Anti-Semitism in Germany during the half-century of Kurt Weill's lifetime—indeed, even long before that—had never been far beneath the surface. The vicious pressure of political events conjured up the image of the Jew as "other," especially in the aftermath of the Holocaust when passions ran high over the Zionist crusade for the establishment of the state of Israel.

I discovered this passage written by Kurt in a letter he sent from America to his mother in Palestine. I found his words revealing—and relevant to what I had been grappling with:

> Religion is a matter of conviction. It can be reached by three paths. The first is that of upbringing and custom, and you have performed a dutiful service by showing us this path. The second path is that of society. The observance of religious practices is made easier by one's membership of a community. I tried to join such a community, and thought I had found friendship in these circles but it was that very community which destroyed that friendship, leaving me

> with a feeling of such profound contempt for the Jewish circles that it is impossible for me to have anything to do with them. The other Jews—the assimilators and Zionists—are in any case totally impossible. So there remains only the third path, namely, to start from the point of one's own development as a human being and gradually find one's way back to the faith of one's childhood.

I reread this passage several times, marveling at its incisiveness, its prescience, its applicability to my life.

The first path that Kurt described, religion by upbringing, was not available to me. As pleased as Kurt seemed to be with his parents for having performed a "dutiful service" in this regard, I had no personal experience with this route—as must be obvious by now. The second path that Kurt mentioned, the feeling of some alienation with the Jewish community, even "contempt," as he described it, was not my path either. While not identifying as Jewish myself, I held no animosity toward the Jewish people as a whole—in fact, quite the opposite. If I'm guilty of anything, it is of subscribing to the usual stereotypes attached to Jews, even while not necessarily accepting them all as accurate, especially the bad ones. More often, I have the reflexive instinct to defend Jewish people against various attacks, to the extent they needed or wanted defending.

But it was Kurt's third path to religion that interested me the most: "to start from the point of one's own development as a human being and gradually find one's way back to the faith of one's childhood." As I read this section of the letter, trying to parse each word, it suddenly occurred to me, slapping me in the face in perhaps the way that I needed it most—without warning—a missile of sorts from one of my ancestors that I never met and, in fact, was just getting to know.

But the words applied to me, there was no denying that. Even if I didn't necessarily have a "faith of one's childhood" that I could "gradually find my way back to," I did have a childhood, and a mother and a father. My parents came from somewhere and so did I. Not a terribly profound recognition but one that seemed to me significant, especially now, as I studied my most well-known relative.

I was finding my way back. Plain and simple. Finding my way back.

Identifying a suitable financial sponsor was key to the emigration prospects of German Jews who were prohibited by Nazi edict from taking their savings with them to America. In order for my family to have been able to get into the United States, there had to be a person of financial means already in the country who could support their emigration.

Who was the one person in our family who could have made that possible?

The answer was obvious: the composer Kurt Weill, my grandfather's first cousin to whom he was quite close.

I have no definitive documentation of this, no official government papers that confirm that this was true. But the more I thought about it, and talked with various individuals who were well-versed in this area, the only plausible conclusion was that there weren't going to be any such documents. My family, in effect, was being put in the front of the line, ahead of others who were trying to get into the country as well but had less means, fewer connections. Maneuvers of this kind were not something that the US government, or Kurt Weill for that matter, would have wanted to be put into writing. So it wasn't. But how my family got to this country in 1939, when the window of opportunity to get out of Germany was narrowing and the door to get into the United States was slamming shut, seems obvious to me.

Without the composer, my family's fate would have been quite different. In fact, I wouldn't be writing these words. So, in many important ways, Kurt Weill was the inflection point in our family's long history, a conduit from the Old Country to the New One, a way for the Weill family to continue, even if in a different form.

As I write these pages, I try to recall what my father said about Kurt Weill—if he even ever uttered a single word about him to me.

There isn't much to remember. Aside from occasionally playing his music, my father seldom spoke of the man. When someone would ask him whether we were related to the composer—at a dinner party or a professional function—my father would brush it off, roll his eyes, shrug his shoulders. I got the distinct impression that my father spent very little time, if any, thinking about Kurt Weill, generally, or the influence that he had our family's destiny life, specifically. This surprised me, in light of my current vantage point, given that it is entirely possible that without Kurt Weill's fame, his connections, his money, immigration to the United States would have not been possible for my father's family. Where they would have ended up otherwise is anyone's guess—if the family would have survived at all. The six-hundred-year run would have been over, not just in Germany, but everywhere.

So as I studied this man and this family, I realized—Kurt Weill was not merely a relative of mine who happened to be famous and little else. No. He was the hinge point for our family's destiny, an inflection that could not be simply dismissed. Kurt Weill may very well be the reason I am here, living this life. I don't consider that hyperbole. I think it is fact. And why my father didn't appreciate that may say something about him—gratitude was a character trait that he struggled with, in spite of his many positive attributes.

My thoughts about this now, though, are simple: I'd like to thank the man. And when someone brings him up to me again—asks if I am related to him at a San Francisco fundraiser or a New York cocktail party, or tells me how important his music was to them—I'll smile and accept the compliment. I'll tell whoever mentions Kurt that I'm proud to be related to him and maybe even tell the story of the role he played in facilitating the survival of our family—and I'll tell Kurt himself if he ever comes to me in my dreams again. I hope he does.

From what I have learned, Kurt Weill was a complicated man, as was my father, as were the other men in my family—perhaps even me, although I am in a poor position to judge. He was introverted, obsessed with his work, and kept his Jewishness at arm's length—all traits of the Weill men I have known, a family phenotype that is unshakable and, at times, unappealing, I am certain. I can also say, although a bit presumptuously, that the more I read of the man, the more we seemed alike, both in ways that are positive and in some that aren't.

My father did stay loosely in touch with Lotte Lenya after Kurt's death in 1950. He told me that he had dinner with her a few times in New York in the 1960s and seventies. I remember, decades ago, asking my father what he and Lotte talked about when they got together. As was typical, he answered, "Not much." And that was that.

But if anyone could understand Kurt Weill, based on my reading, it seems as though Lotte had the best chance to do so. But even she struggled, apparently.

"There was always a wall around him," she said the year before she died. "People never really knew him. And I'm not sure I ever really knew him, even after twenty-four years of marriage and the two years we lived together before that. And when he died, I looked at him and asked myself, did I ever really love him?"

Lotte Lenya died in 1981 and is buried next to Kurt in Mt. Repose, a nondenominational cemetery in Haverstraw, New York, which is north of the City. With Lotte's passing, any personal connection of the composer to our family was gone. I only wish I could have met him somewhere other than in my dreams.

But a relative that I didn't just meet while asleep, my most significant influence IRL (in real life), as my daughters would say, was my father, a man I only partly understood—until now.

CHAPTER SIX

HANS WEILL, MY FATHER

Germany, Florida, New Orleans, 1933–2013

The author and his father, Hans Weill, New Orleans, 1964

MY FATHER SURE KNEW HOW TO MAKE AN ENTRANCE.

Nineteen thirty-three was an eventful year in German history. Adolf Hitler became chancellor on January 30 of that year and immediately began instituting anti-Jewish measures, including the boycott of Jewish-owned businesses on April 1, 1933. My father was born soon after in August 1933.

A couple of years later in 1935, the Nuremberg racial laws were passed and the writing was on the wall, if the German plan for the Jewish people was not yet readily apparent. The Nazis began to mandate that Jews have a J stamped on their passports, and required the addition of Israel and Sarah as middle names on these official documents.

If the signals were interpreted as murky by some, very few had any remaining doubt that the Jewish people were in mortal danger when Kristallnacht occurred in November of 1938, after which thirty thousand Jews were incarcerated in places like Buchenwald and Dachau.

After my grandfather's arrest and imprisonment at Buchenwald and his subsequent immigration to the United States in September of 1938, my father, his mother, and brother were forced to wait in Berlin until February of 1939 to finally leave Germany to be reunited with their father and husband. Their departure marked the end of the Weill Family in Germany—and the start of the Weill Family in the United States.

When my grandparents and father moved to Miami, what did they find?

My father's family quickly followed the blueprint that immigrants have traditionally used to establish a new life in America: hard work, close attention to the academic life of their two sons, and, of course, finding an expat community that had similar interests and cultural values. With a significant European Jewish immigrant population, South Florida became a comfortable, if still somewhat foreign, place for my father's family. Multiple languages could be heard on the streets, and inside my father's boyhood home. My grandparents spoke German to one another—at the dinner table, at the kitchen table late at night—but they insisted that their two boys only speak English to each other and anyone else they encountered. It would make them seem less foreign, my father explained to me years later, less "other."

My father told me several times over the years that he didn't know any English when he came to the United States, immediately thrown into an elementary school that made no accommodation for his language deficiency. When I asked him once while I was in high school how he managed that situation, one where he sat in classes trying to decipher what was being taught, he gave a response that was typical of his attitude regarding just about everything: "I figured it out."

My father and I talked nearly every day, throughout his life, up until he slipped into a coma soon before his death. We spent hours on the phone covering a vast array of topics, sometimes even when I had patients waiting on me. We covered every conceivable topic, at least those originating in the left brain: medicine, global affairs, movies, football, books we had read—and then, sadly toward the end, nearly exclusively his health.

I asked him once when I was much older, a grown man with a family of my own, when I would have secretly liked to carry his name after he was gone, why he didn't name me Hans? "I wouldn't do that to you." That was all he said, but I know what he meant. He wanted me as assimilated as possible, to be even slightly WASPy, if that were possible, anything that might make me stick out less, instead of "other," more like "another." He was like other Holocaust survivors in that way. Their children would not be exposed to what they were exposed to—not now, not ever.

* * *

As a boy, my father became obsessed with the war, he told me. Even at his young age, he devoured the newspaper every day, following the progress of the Allied troops using a map and a set of push pins to see how close the Germans were to defeat. He understood well what the Nazis had done to his family, so he tracked the Allies' advance, all the way up to V-J Day in August 1945, a day my father would always remember.

His family was on a trip to North Carolina, a tradition that began as a way to escape the brutal heat of the South Florida summers. On that historic day, there were celebrations of all sorts, with drinking and dancing—my father recalled having his first taste of champagne at age twelve. More astonishing, given my family's roots and my father and grandfather's view of religion, they went to church when the war ended. My grandfather was even called out by the Baptist congregation to say a few words about what the end of the war meant to him. My father recalled that, when he spoke in the church, he sounded just like Henry Kissinger but with a heavier German accent. My grandfather's comments centered around how well the people of the United States had treated his family, which likely explained my father's fervent patriotism that he displayed throughout his life.

It wasn't until more than twenty years later that my father, grandfather, and uncle could face visiting Germany—a trip that my father said was filled with lingering resentment and anxiety, even though the war had concluded years before. Their experience in Nazi Germany was something that could not be forgotten. There would be no "turning of the page," no "moving on." The family had lost part of themselves in Germany—and there would be no getting it back.

After only a few days in Berlin, my grandfather, uncle, and father decided to leave, returning to the United States with no intention of ever going back to the country of their birth.

Despite the bumpy start, my father looked back on his Miami Beach youth with fondness. As he grew older, he worked after school at the small diner that my grandparents opened in Miami Beach, tending to the bar and learning the ins and outs of being a soda jerk, or as his father kidded him, "a soda jerk without the soda part."

Meanwhile, in addition to running the diner, Kurt worked his way up at various restaurants, first as a busboy, then a chef, and ultimately a manager. He went on to manage restaurants at a few prominent beach hotels, where his wife, Gerda, would perform hostess duties after her day at the preschool was done. My father would help out at these restaurants as well, hustling home from school to perform a number of jobs: waiter, room service, and bartender.

If the weekdays were busy with school and the diner, my father's weekends were filled with one main activity: going to the beach. An avid swimmer, my father built his social life around the beach that was only a few blocks from the family home. Meeting friends, trying to draw the attention of the girls there, swimming out through the waves in the Atlantic Ocean—my father reveled in all that Florida had to offer.

After high school, my father enrolled as a pre-medical student at the University of Florida in Gainesville, but he didn't stay there long. In the first few days after his arrival, he received a letter from Tulane University saying that he was the recipient of a full academic scholarship. Weighing his options, my father made a quick decision and boarded a bus to New Orleans.

* * *

What did my father find in New Orleans?

In short, a tapestry that has, for centuries, enthralled visitors and locals alike. Distinctive food, music, architecture, people—it was all there. But in no area are the divergent influences in New Orleans more apparent than in its religious heterogeneity.

A Jewish Legacy

The Jewish community in New Orleans began with the arrival of a Dutch Sephardic Jew, Isaac Monsanto, in 1724, just a few years after the French establishment of the colony. Among the early Jewish group was Judah Touro, a wildly successful businessman and merchant who became a generous philanthropist. To this day in New Orleans, Touro Hospital, Touro Street, and Touro Synagogue still bear his name. In the mid-nineteenth century, the Sephardim were joined by immigrant Jews from Germany and the French region of Alsace-Lorraine, interestingly, the area from which my family originated.

I knew of this multigenerational Jewish presence in New Orleans as a young man but also was keenly aware of the prominent presence of a strong WASPy influence, best embodied by the country clubs and debutante parties, and Mardi Gras Krewes, which are blue-blood organizations that essentially sponsor the entire Mardi Gras party for the rest of the city—its loyal subjects, if you will. The most well-established of these organizations is called Rex. I was surprised to find out as I did my research that the first Krewe of Rex's King of Carnival in 1872 was a Jew—the businessman Louis Solomon, who eventually converted to Episcopalianism. That surprised me, a former Jew attaining such a prestigious social position. He was also, in fact, a founding member of the exclusive Boston Club, a somewhat secretive luncheon club that parallels Rex in social importance.

But things changed in the early twentieth century as the new Jewish arrivals from Germany increased the complexity of the community, expanding from a few socially accepted Sephardic Jews to an increasing numbers of German Jewish immigrants. Exclusion by the elite Mardi Gras Krewes and clubs became the norm. Then, as now, the Krewes are where the top of the city's power structure resides.

The new wave of Jews from Germany and Alsace-Lorraine became successful businessmen, notably cotton brokers and department store owners, and continued Touro's philanthropic pattern. The legacy of Jewish philanthropy has been a significant aspect of life in New Orleans and examples abound of the community's generosity, whether it be toward education, healthcare, or the arts.

Arriving a day after classes started, my father quickly adjusted to his new surroundings in a part of the country that he had never been, but one that intrigued him and a place that he would eventually call home for many decades.

My father plowed on with his pre-medical studies, putting the grief associated with his mother's death aside and going on to achieve an outstanding academic record. Nonetheless, he was rejected to Tulane Medical School on his first try in 1953. How did I know this? Not because he told me, but rather because after his death I found the rejection letter in a small box that contained precious few other documents. But he saved this one. In the urban lexicon of today, he "kept receipts."

I asked my mother recently if she knew anything about the impact this had on him, and why he had been rejected.

"Oh, because he was Jewish," my mother said.

"Because he was Jewish?" I asked with some degree of astonishment. I thought to myself, *a Jewish undergraduate, rejected to med school at Tulane of all places, because he was Jewish?*

"Yeah," my mother said. "Remember it was 1958, not today." Then she looked toward the ceiling, clearly trying to remember something, a habit she had formed in recent years. "He applied again the following year . . . and I think he got a board member to help him. But I don't remember the rest."

My father, strings being pulled to help him get into medical school, after being rejected because he was Jewish? Academic failure? Him?

None of that really comported with what I knew of my father, but, in a vast understatement, a great deal about his life was left unsaid.

I suspect the whole experience of being rejected, unfairly it seems, was something that fueled his will to try even harder in his professional life—to do better, to be better. My father didn't accept rejection. *That was for other people,* he used to say to me, even when I was a young boy.

But there was more to my father's story, as I would find out long after he died—and I got to hear it in his own words.

By an unusual and devastating set of circumstances, after my father's death, I got a complete recounting of his childhood experience. How so? From a recorded interview that he did with my niece Katy for a school project when she was thirteen—and several years before her own tragic death at twenty-one.

My sister Leslie gave me the tape after I told her I was working on this book. She handed me the microcassette: "You may want to listen to this." I bought the right type of recorder at an office supply company, placed the batteries inside and turned it on in my home office. Our house had emptied out that morning as it did most mornings, leaving me with a lit candle on my desk and two labradoodles at my feet.

The quality of the recording was poor; not surprising since the interview had been conducted by a middle school kid nearly a decade ago. Poor sound quality or not, I was still taken aback by hearing the voices of two people who were no longer around, two family members who had died, one old, one young, missing pieces from a family that wasn't large to begin with.

After going through a few bits of background—my father's parents' names, the trip to visit the hospital when my father's younger brother Peter was born—Katy asked about the night my grandfather was taken away. "It was the middle of the night, there was a knock on the door. Several. It was loud. And then he was gone. My mother didn't say where he went. As a kid, you know, you didn't have any idea." My father said it as a matter of fact, in some ways like he was talking about someone else, which might be understandable given how much time had passed.

He did say that after his father left, he remembered being scared nearly all the time during the six-month period before my father, his brother, and their mother would sail to America—a long journey that was fraught with fear and uncertainty.

Then he laughed a little. "But the worst part was the seasickness on the Queen Mary on the way to the United States. I threw up for a week!" Just then, I stopped the tape and smiled, remembering all the times when my father would take me out on our small boat into the Gulf of Mexico off the Florida coast. The boat would bounce all over the place, and when I told him I was about to vomit, he would say "Look out at the horizon—that helps." Maybe he knew from experience. By the way, it never helped. But he did teach me to throw up off the back so flecks of my puke wouldn't hit him in the face while he drove the boat.

Katy then asked about my grandfather's release from Buchenwald. "Were you happy?" she asked.

"Oh yeah. Relieved," my father said. "But then he soon went to the train station to leave the country. That was September of 1938. So we were without him once again—and weren't sure when we would see him. If we would see him . . ." my father's voice trailed off. I couldn't tell if it was the tape quality or just a moment of reflection. "My father was thirty-six at the time. I was five."

Katy and my father went on to talk about other aspects of his life, parts that I have already discussed in this book. Still, I listened to the recording over and over, trying to see if I could glean any additional meaning from my father's words, any nuances that I might have missed, any tone or texture that might be revealing.

As it was on this recording, my father's German-ness was nearly always on full display—his discipline, his love of order, his punctuality—and his expectation of those of us around him to be on time. His Jewishness, on the other hand, came out in dribbles, inconsistently, at unexpected times—the odd reference to a famous person being Jewish or, my father's favorite, references to the intellectual prowess of Jews. An anglophile from his time spent doing research in the UK, one of his favorite sayings—one he repeated to me as a boy many times—was, "Think Yiddish and dress British."

Later that day, after listening to his voice for the first time in a decade, I considered my role in his life. While it is natural for a boy to consider his father a hero, it seemed that as I grew older, the opposite may have been true. I was his hero. I could do things he could never do, had opportunities that he never had, all because I didn't have the profound challenges that he had early in life. I was secure and happy, because of circumstance, yes, but also because of the life afforded to me by my parents. So even when my father needed a liver transplant, there I was, a transplant doctor, greasing the wheel so that could happen successfully.

My father never expressed the way he felt about me, not admiration, gratitude for what I did to help him, or even professions of love. It was implied certainly, but whether because of his German-ness or his generation, it was all left unsaid. I wasn't looking for an outpouring of emotion from him. I knew that wasn't his way, but maybe I needed it—and it's something I do differently with my daughters, frequently telling them how special they are, how much I love them. Perhaps I've overcorrected in the opposite direction, but playing the role of my father's hero and protector, in many ways, was a difficult burden to carry—and one I didn't understand until recently. I'll avoid that dynamic with my daughters, Hannah and Ava.

Satisfied that there was nothing more, I gave the cassette back to my sister the next day. I suspected she would want to have it.

Now that I had more information, the result of hours of reading and conversation, contemplation and rumination, what did it all mean, for my family—and for me?

PART THREE

INHERITANCE

An underrated symptom of inherited trauma is how socially awkward it is to live with.

—*The Ministry of Time* by Kaliane Bradley

Leopoldstadt *playing at Longacre on Broadway, 2023*

CHAPTER ONE

LEOPOLDSTADT

New York, 2022

In December of 2022, my wife Jackie and I decided to take a holiday trip to New York for a few days. Joining us would be our longtime friend, Robert David, who is the rare individual in a married couple's life: He is equally good friends with both husband and wife. A former naval aviator, and now a pilot for Homeland Security, Robert feels comfortable doing guy things with me: working out, going to cigar bars, and watching college football on Saturday afternoons. He also feels comfortable shopping with Jackie and having long lunches, neither of which is my strong suit.

But on this trip, one of the first decisions the three of us had was what play to see. My mind was made up early: I wanted to see Tom Stoppard's *Leopoldstadt.* The play is about the Merz family from Vienna, followed over several decades, through good times and bad. The themes of the play center around the role of Judaism in the family's life—and how their perception of their own Jewishness changed as society changed. I read the rave reviews in *The New York Times* and the subject matter certainly resonated with me, but not so much with Jackie and Robert. Together they reviewed other options, looking for theater times that would roughly coincide with the Saturday matinee of *Leopoldstadt*. They chose *MJ: The Musical*, featuring a collection of Michael Jackson's greatest hits.

Before the play, the three of us made our way to a crowded theater district lunch spot a friend had recommended, enjoying casual conversation over the bustle of the restaurant. But as we chatted, I sensed that I was going to have quite a different experience later that afternoon than Jackie and Robert. As we waited for our food, I wondered if I had made the right decision and even briefly considered bagging my original plans all together and going online to purchase a last minute ticket to the MJ show.

But that thought came and then was gone. Off we went to our respective shows, walking in the cold drizzle, me to the Longacre Theater, turning off on West 48th street, and Jackie and Robert to the Neil Simon Theater on West 52nd Street.

I sat down in my seat a few minutes before the show was set to start and had a look around. It was an older crowd—perhaps because it was the matinee, or maybe due to the subject matter of the play. I noticed right away that there were other people there by themselves. I have never been self-conscious about being in public places by myself—whether at a restaurant, a movie, or at a hotel bar. It's just a part of a life spent traveling for work.

But as the play was about to start, I was acutely aware of my "aloneness." This time, this day, this play was mine to enjoy (*is that the right word?*) alone. It was time to absorb the material, in all its nuances and in all its relevance to me, in solitude. It seemed right, even if the Michael Jackson musical might have made for a lighter afternoon—one more cheerful, less intense, but also likely less meaningful.

The curtain came up.

As the play went on, the parallel tracks of Stoppard's characters and my own family became obvious: a long ancestral history in a specific region of Europe, the younger generations' ambivalence about their religious identity—and religion in general—and the profound disruption of familial roots that came during the Nazi era. But what struck me the most occurred toward the end of the play, when the war was over, and those who were left had to put their lives back together. It became clear that with this family—and my own—there wouldn't be any "moving on," that the trauma they all endured would remain beyond any single generation that directly experienced the brunt of it.

And then—the final scene that hit me the hardest—the dialogue between Leo and Rosa while looking at a family tree in the 1950s:

> Leo: Eva.
> Rosa: She died on the transport, 1943.
> Leo: Ludwig.
> Rosa: Steinhof, 1941

And then more.

> Leo: Hanna
> Rosa: Auschwitz
> Leo: Kurt
> Rosa: Dachau, 1938

Leo: Zacharia
Rosa: Death march. Nowhere.
Leo: Sally
Rosa: Auschwitz

And on. And on . . .
The curtain came down.

When the play ended, I was motionless, paralyzed, my hand clutching a tissue that I kept out through the entire play. The lights now on, I could see that I wasn't the only one stuck in my chair quietly crying. I stayed that way for several minutes, trying to process what I just witnessed. I looked to my right and saw an elderly couple holding each other's hand, still, silent.

After most of the audience had filed out, I decided to leave. I shuffled past a woman about my age who was seated in my row. As I went by, she gave me a half-smile. I smiled back, having a moment that one sometimes shares with strangers after such an intense theater experience. All she said as I looked at her was, "Well . . ."

Yes, well. I put my hand on her shoulder as I moved past.

I made my way out to the street, moving slowly toward Broadway. It was still raining, but I didn't feel like hailing a taxi. I wanted to move around, get some fresh air, even if I was getting soaked. I walked south toward my hotel in SoHo. And kept walking all the way back, an hour's journey in all. Thoughts swirled through my head, blocking out the traffic noise, the holiday street buzz that was even louder than usual. I didn't hear any of it.

My father, his father, the hundreds of years of rabbis in the family, the knock on my grandfather's door, Buchenwald, and the little boy, my father, on the Queen Mary, *seasick and scared.*

All of it washed over me as I picked up the pace, drenched but determined to get back to my hotel, to the people I loved, my wife and one of my best friends, to make the connection after what I witnessed at the theater. I was thankful for the experience that I just had, and for the time to process it on the way south on that cold, rainy day in Manhattan.

Stolperstein, Berlin, 2023

CHAPTER TWO

BERLIN

November 2023

I'D SEEN OTHER PEOPLE CRY ON A PLANE BEFORE, AND THE reasons varied. I had witnessed couples breaking up (many times for some reason), adult children on their way to a parent's funeral, young parents on the way to get treatment for their child with cancer, tears shed in close quarters. But those kinds of public displays of emotion? Never happened to me. Not once. Until now.

I was on a return flight from Berlin, the city of my father's birth, after having spent a few days there with my older daughter, Hannah, who was in college and studying in Spain that semester. She had visited nearly every major European city with her friends over the previous few months, using Barcelona as a launching point from which she left almost every Thursday, returning Sunday sleep-deprived and moderately hungover. I joked with her on our daily calls that it seemed she was using her classes as something to occupy her in between trips—and that the phrase "studying abroad" should be dropped from the English lexicon.

We decided, even before she left home for Europe, that we would do a father-daughter trip to the place where my family lived up until they were forced to flee the country, escaping in February 1939 just before the proverbial door shut. I had been to Berlin once before, just a few months after the Wall came down in 1990. At that tumultuous time, and because my family had history there, I wanted to be there, to feel it, to see what insight I could glean from breathing the same air my father and his father once did.

During that trip, I traipsed around the city in the cold, wet rain, seeing what I could but missing my father's presence, his ability to put into context some of what I was seeing, to attach meaning to the city, and, perhaps most importantly, to understand how he felt about what happened there so many years ago. I didn't have many opportunities like this to understand my father's emotions. Really, none at all. As it turned out, this was not going to be one of those times, so I did the exploring on my own—a metaphor for how I would live the rest of my life as it related to understanding my family's past.

But this trip with Hannah, I thought on the way over the Atlantic, would be an opportunity to touch the place, not with my father as I had hoped—he had died ten years prior—but instead a way for me to have a different experience with Hannah, who was just beginning to learn about Germany, the Holocaust, and all things Weill. I thought the trip would be meaningful, but mainly just fun, one of the few chances I had to be one on one with my older daughter.

Which it was. But I was shocked by how deeply affected I was by the trip as I sat on the plane on the way home, having to cover my face with a lunch napkin after quickly going through the tiny tissue packs the airline provided. The flight attendant, desperately trying to help, asked if I needed a doctor. "I am a doctor . . . although that's not helping me much at the moment." She patted my hand and walked back toward the galley, leaving me to wonder—not for the first time—what was going on with me. But more precisely, what had happened in Berlin?

I had landed at Brandenburg Airport just five days prior on a clear but cold early November morning. I was still in a fog, brought on by the time difference, red wine, half an Ambien, and only a precious few hours of fitful sleep.

"What brings you to Berlin?" the driver asked, looking at me through the rearview mirror of his sedan. I could see from the placard on the dashboard that his name was Ahmad.

What brings me to Berlin?

"Meeting my daughter," I said, too tired to elaborate further. I watched the industrial part of the city go by, the nondescript factories, the post-war office buildings. Berlin was just waking up, rush hour traffic still not at its peak.

What brings me to Berlin? I considered the question some more.

Meeting my relatives, I thought, *my past.*

I knew the reason. I just didn't know what I would find there.

I stood on the street in front of my hotel, welcoming the fresh early-morning air after the long flight from Newark.

I had booked a room at the Hotel Adlon, one of the most iconic hotels in Europe. It opened in 1907 and was mostly destroyed in 1945 during the closing days of World War II. I chose to stay there because of its location, yes—out its back door was the Memorial to the Murdered Jews of Europe—but also because it was a place of historical significance, the most important trait I look for in a hotel, more so than the availability of twenty-four-hour room service, a well-stocked minibar, or a modern fitness facility, although I like having all those, too. The hotel is located on Unter Der Linden—the main boulevard in the central Mitte district—directly opposite the Brandenburg Gate, and was the preferred Nazi gathering spot for both social and political events.

On this cloudless November morning, the tourists had just started to gather at the gate. Large groups were led by tour guides with raised flags. Some were school-aged students using their phones to take pictures, even if they were unsure what they were looking at. Others were older tourists who likely knew exactly what they were seeing. Directly across the street from the hotel, the young and old filed in and out of a Starbucks. I watched the people leave the coffee shop, all with identical paper cups embossed with the familiar logo, marching down the street with their caffeine fix.

But I saw something else as well—not in reality, not on the famous boulevard in the year 2023, but in my imagination. I saw huge crowds cheering uniformed men with swastikas on their arms, an image I recalled from a black-and-white photograph that I had seen in a book. It was a nighttime photo from the Nazi era, ominous when I looked at it in two dimensions, but even more foreboding as I stood in the very spot where the German Army marched eighty years ago. I fixated on that image for a moment, thinking about what it must have felt like that night, wondering what was in the air—excitement? fear? blood thirst?

And now there was a Starbucks and, nearby, a modern building next to the Brandenburg Gate that was the US Embassy, and Japanese schoolchildren—and me. I just stood there, blinking, wondering how we got from there to here in just a generation.

Time marches on, as the saying goes. Or does it? Somehow, in my life at least, time—and the past—doesn't just seem to march on. Especially here in Berlin. Not for me.

When I checked with the front desk, my room wasn't ready yet. The person at the hotel registration desk helpfully reminded me that check-in was "precisely" at 3:00 p.m.

"Thank you," I said, "for the precision." I smiled slightly. Stereotypical German traits always reminded me of my father, who I dearly missed.

My bags safely stored away with the bellman, I walked out of the hotel and buttoned my coat against the damp air. After the long journey, I was glad to be on the move.

I headed east, slowly shaking off the jet lag as I looked for the Hackenstrasse section, my father's boyhood neighborhood. Described online as "Berlin's Brooklyn," home to the young and the hip, I found it hard to imagine that it was the same area where my father's family had lived. These days, hipsters attracted by the thriving tech industry come from all over the world to Berlin, indulging in the art and nightlife, hanging out during the day in cafes that dot each block.

Several blocks along, I turned sharply into an alley that caught my attention. There was art on the walls in vibrant colors revealing street scenes and murals of historical figures, including an especially vivid one of a smiling Anne Frank. Even at this hour, techno beats wafted out of nearby clubs, providing the soundtrack for the men cleaning up the previous night's mess inside.

Back out on the main street, I pulled out one of my business cards, where the address was written on the back.

11 Raupachstrasse. My father's boyhood home.

The dry goods shop that my grandparents owned, and the cellar below, were next door, my father had once told me. "Convenient so my parents could close up shop and have lunch at home," he said.

I kept walking, past the Apple and Fendi stores, where I took a left and went a few blocks, right past Sammie's Doughnut Shop. And then I started to notice the small plaques embedded in the cobblestone sidewalks, in front of every other house, it seemed.

Avril Strauss, Deported Aug 3, 1941.

Then, *Sarah Levy, Deported October 9, 1939.* And so on. The plaques stretched out for blocks, small gold plaques, some single, some in clusters, stretched out down the street, like stepping stones to my family's past. I found out before the trip that these were called Stolperstein, translated literally as "stumbling stone," and metaphorically as "stumbling block"—an interpretation that certainly seemed apt to me on this day.

I read them quickly as I went by, my pace quickening as I got closer to the address I had written down.

> *Primo Hochstein, Deported June 9, 1942.*
> *Annabelle Appleman, Deported December 19, 1943.*

Where was 11 Raupachstrasse?

I glanced up at the steep façades of the houses as I passed them, my pace quickening, almost to a light jog. After a few blocks, I dropped to a knee and unzipped the front compartment of my backpack. I took out the faded black-and-white photograph of my father and his parents, sitting on the front steps, my grandfather shielding the sunlight from his eyes, my father sitting on my grandmother's lap, smiling for the camera. I turned it over. Written in pencil that was now barely discernible was *1937.*

I flipped the photo back over and looked up at the vertical buildings rising toward the gray sky. Where was it? I passed a few more Stolpersteins that were similar to the others, but none with my last name.

Leo Siegel, Deported September 17, 1942. I went down on one knee and ran my hand over it—slowly tracing the name on the plaque, drawing out the S in Siegel with my right index finger. Pedestrians fast-walked by me, on their way to work presumably. I figured many of these people had seen this before, another Jewish visitor looking for their ancestral home, another mourner on his knees, connecting to a past that one could never really comprehend, no matter how hard one tried. "Excuse me," a passing man said in German-accented English as he walked around me.

I stood up, rubbing the palms of my hands. My eyes burned—*Was it the overnight flight? Was it being in the neighborhood? Was it the Stolperstein?* For a man who was paid not to crack, who made a profession of maintaining composure, the emotions I was feeling now were not my own. As I searched another hour for my father's home, I was oblivious to the cars honking, the people talking on the streets, the construction crews erecting another modern building in this bustling city. Instead, I thought only of my ancestors whose house was invaded, my grandfather yanked out of bed, pulled to the street in front of 11 Raupachstrasse, and sent off to a distant camp, perhaps to die—perpetrators of "crimes" that neither they nor any sane person could possibly understand.

I had one last look around the neighborhood. I came to the conclusion, sadly, that the house in the photograph was no longer there. The antique store that had been next door, and presumably the cellar beneath it, were gone, replaced with a convenience store that sold lottery tickets and cigarettes. I went into the store, had a look around, and asked the elderly man behind the counter for a bottle of water. "Pack of gum?" he asked.

No, I said.

Unsmiling, he asked for two euros.

I walked back in the direction of the hotel still trying to process what I had seen, and not seen—my father's house that I couldn't find. I zigzagged past museums, a university, and T-shirt shops lining the street leading back to the hotel. I slowed my pace down. I needed to think.

When I got back to the hotel, the lobby was full of well-dressed men and women in business suits, nearly indistinguishable from one another. There was a sign that read *Premier Capital Meeting*, with an arrow pointing down a wide, well-lit hallway leading to the back of the hotel.

I stopped at the registration desk and asked if my room was ready. "Doctor Weill (*Doctor Vile*, it sounded like, sadly), I am pleased to report that your room is ready." The young man behind the desk presented my plastic room card on a silver platter, as if holding rare caviar. "I trust you enjoyed your walk around our beautiful—and very modern—city."

Modern.

And not modern. A city with a past, a dark past, my family's past.

Hannah arrived later that first night, and my relief when we reunited startled me a bit. She had a calming influence on me, especially after a day that was anything but calm. After we chatted for a bit about school, her travels, her friends, we talked about what we would do over the next few days. She took out her computer and opened a document she had created with *Berlin* written at the top. Hannah had become an intrepid traveler over the last few months, and it filled me with pride and joy to see her take charge in formulating the plan for our trip.

On our second day in Berlin, Hannah and I visited the Empty Library, or *Bibliothek*. The Library is a public memorial created by Israeli sculptor Micha Ullman, dedicated to the remembrance of the Nazi book burnings that took place in the Bebelplatz. It is simple but moving, a collection of empty, subterranean bookcases set beneath the cobblestones of the plaza.

The book burnings took place on May 10, 1933, on a dreary, rainy evening, as forty thousand people crowded into the public square to watch German students hold burning torches and ignite piles of books that had been seized for the event. Joseph Goebbels, the German Minister for Popular Enlightenment and Propaganda, spoke at the event, declaring that "the era of exaggerated Jewish intellectualism is now at an end . . . and the future German man will not just be a man of books . . . this late hour [I] entrust to the flames the intellectual garbage of the past." Thirty-four more book burnings would take place across Germany later that month.

Hannah and I stood at the edge of the glass and peered down into the memorial. "Books," she asked. "What were they so afraid of?"

I shrugged, a reasonable question. "Knowledge, a different point of view," I said. "Books are powerful, a way to influence, to present ideas to the masses. Not scary if you believe in a free society. Unacceptable if you don't." I thought just then of what was happening back in our own country—not eighty years ago, but right now—with some calling for the banning of books addressing LBGTQIA+ and racial issues, climate change, and the Holocaust.

I put my arm around her. "Let's find a bookstore." She smiled. We were a reading family. I inherited that trait from my mother. Jackie read to the kids each night before bedtime when they were young. As Hannah and I walked away, arm in arm, we noticed a bronze plaque inlaid into the cobblestones a few feet away. A quote from the German Jewish author Heinrich Heine's play *Almansor* was etched into one of the stones:

> *That was but a prelude;*
> *where they burn books,*
> *they will ultimately burn people as well*

Hannah and I looked at the words on the plaque in silence. I reread the quote a few times, then looked at her. I could sense that she was starting to get it, what had happened, to them, to us.

There was nothing more to say, so we started walking toward a nearby bookstore.

Having a glass of wine in the hotel lobby while I waited for Hannah to get ready for dinner, I spoke to a Ukrainian waitress who wanted desperately to try out her English on me. "Go ahead," I said. "We won't get far on my Ukrainian."

She smiled and launched in. "One other red wine?"

"Better said, 'One more red wine.' One other red wine might give someone the idea you were asking if they wanted to switch to a different type of wine." I don't know why I was encouraging her to be so precise with her English, since she spoke it a lot better than my Ukrainian or any other foreign language for that matter.

"Ah, yes. So then . . . one more red wine?"

"Perfect. Yes, but it might not just be one more."

"Like a Russian, no?" Not a compliment, I was sure. At the time,

Russia was well into its brutal war with her home country, littered with daily atrocities, only a small fraction of which had already been revealed. There would be more to come.

I laughed. "Not like a Russian. My family's German. My father's family moved to the United States when he was young."

She raised her eyebrows, replacing my cocktail napkin with a dry one. "Smart."

"Yep, smart. Lucky," I said.

"My family too. My grandparents were killed in the pogroms. The Nazis came to their village and then," she snapped her fingers, "all gone."

I nodded as she shrugged, then walked off. Collective pain, the world over.

Over the next couple of days, we visited the same places that so many others had. Given that it was directly behind the hotel, we went first to the Holocaust Memorial, also called the Memorial to the Murdered Jews of Europe—a literal name that struck me as so descriptive and so German. The irregular cement blocks, while open to anyone's interpretation, looked like giant coffins to me. Next was the Reichstag, then the Tiergarten, and, of course, one of only two remaining sections of the Berlin Wall that had once divided the East from the West. At the end of the third day, we breezed through Checkpoint Charlie as quickly as we could, put off by all the tourists, the Kentucky Fried Chicken outlet, and the tacky souvenir stores where one could buy a fake piece of the Wall that was even adorned with fake graffiti. The whole scene looked more like Times Square than anything of historical significance, an example of raw commercialization diminishing a place of profound importance.

* * *

After saying our goodbyes, Hannah and I went our separate ways, she to a flight back to Barcelona, me to a plane back to the States. My flight back home would stop in Newark, then after a few hours, go on to New Orleans.

As I settled into the plane, I waited for the other passengers to board. I took out my backpack, placing my iPad and earbuds in the compartment in front of me. I had picked up an English version of Albert Speer's *Inside the Third Reich* from a bookstore in the Mitte section of town. It is a firsthand account of Hitler's madness from one of his closest confidants—a matter-of-fact accounting by Speer of the barbaric behavior, described in ways that tended toward the defensive and self-serving. Before I started reading, I pulled the photograph of my father's home from my backpack and looked at it for perhaps the hundredth time in the last few days.

And it was only then that I completely lost it.

I had held it together for the last few days, through the deeply disturbing concentration camp photos, through the images near the Wall that documented the rise of the Nazis, through watching each gold plaque move under my feet as I walked the sidewalks of Hackenstrasse. But now, on the plane, I was a mess, crying my eyes out, desperate for a tissue, a shirtsleeve, a napkin, anything to wipe the tears running down my face. The person sitting next to me, a German businessman, perhaps, in a suit and tightly knotted tie, busied himself with his laptop, desperate it seemed, to look the other way.

"Is there something that I can get you?" the flight attendant came up and asked. She was around my age with short blond hair. "A tissue, please, maybe wine later," I quipped, trying to laugh it off, my condition. “Never a bad call,” she said, as she handed me a small package of tissues from her smock.

During the long flight, she periodically sat on the armrest of my seat, each of us taking turns telling our story. Her name was Joan, and she grew up in Wisconsin. Her father had fought in World War II in the Pacific Theater, she said, after I told her about my family. “He never said a word about it,” she said, replacing my empty plastic water bottle with a new one, “even when I asked.”

I blew my nose. “Well, I never asked my father, for some reason, about all that”—I waved my hand back at Germany. “I guess I wanted to pretend that wasn’t his past. And not mine either.”

“It’s all of our pasts,” she said. “Whether we talk about it or not.” She had a point. Once again, collective pain.

Somewhere over Iceland, I finally stopped crying. Now it was time to assess what just happened, a very “doctor” thing of me to do.

What was going on?

A great deal, I thought. The horror of it all, of course: the mass slaughter of *a people*, not just a group of people. I pictured my father again and again as a boy, with all the turmoil around him—neighbors disappearing in the night, stores being forced to close, lives shattered. Then I thought of him on the night it happened, when the authorities came and took my grandfather away, for processing first, and then off to Buchenwald. The look on my father’s face, as a little boy, a look I didn’t see except in the imaginative reel running inside my head. Why at such a young age? I couldn’t stop thinking about it. Why was he subjected to that, why was anyone?

And then the guilt came through for growing up the way I did—comfortable, suburban, secure. My father was the way he was, I thought, because of that night, a trauma that affected him deeply for the rest of his life. How could it not? It wasn't a chip on his shoulder about the unfairness of it all, it was a boulder. And I don't think he ever got rid of that boulder. I think it went in the grave with him.

Which made me think of my own life, of course. How could it not?

The privilege, the lack of security concerns, the carefree existence—at least until recently, when I began to explore so much about where and from whom I was descended.

The tears came, because I felt that little boy's pain—my father's—but there was also some shame in it, because as his son, the beneficiary of what he provided, I didn't have to endure it. I wasn't tested in that way. And yes, that might mean I was soft, at least compared to him. I didn't want him to think of me that way—*did he even?*—and I sure as hell didn't want to think of myself that way.

More than anything, though, in that airplane seat, ten years almost to the day after his death, I missed my father—the usual father-son stuff, the conversations, the guidance, the times when we seemed more alike than different. There were long, sunny days at the beach when I was young—swimming together, throwing the football—and sports events we attended when he let me have my first taste of beer. Then later, the career advice he gave me, well thought out and on point.

But still, I didn't know enough about him, how he felt about what happened to him in Germany, and then in the early days in America, how it affected him. I didn't ask, and he wasn't saying, not unprompted, perhaps not even prompted. He wasn't that sort of guy, the kind to reveal. He wasn't a modern man who showed emotion. He was none of those things. My father would not have written any of the words on these pages. Not a single one. He was German. I was an American in the age of the Great Reveal—on social media, in therapists' offices, and yes, on the written page.

So, on the plane that day, returning from Berlin alone, my precious daughter on her way back to Spain, there was nothing left to do but cry; an uncontrollable, whole-body sobbing attack that left me exhausted well after I finally stopped. I thought for a moment, then took out my phone and took a selfie—one of the few times I ever had—so that I could remember this day, this feeling. I wanted to hold on to it, a photo right next to the ones at the beach and of my family, and videos of our dogs. I will never delete that picture.

I had left Berlin, at least the physical part of me had. But it was in me, a part of the DNA my father had passed on to me. I could no more get rid of it than I could my eye color, the way I walked like my father, the way I heard myself talk like him in conversation, the hand gestures, the facial expressions, the body language. These things would never leave me, just like Berlin wouldn't.

And I didn't want it to.

Nazi Germany passport of Kurt Weill, the author's grandfather, 1938

CHAPTER THREE

INHERITED TRAUMA

New Orleans, 2024

NATURE AND NURTURE.

So much has been written about the complex interplay between our biology, on the one hand, and the countless experiences one has during a long life, on the other. I set off on this journey because I wanted to understand more about why I was so interested in my ancestors' plight and the impact that had on what I was feeling—and most importantly, why it all mattered to me.

But as I've studied inheritance, in all its messy forms, I have come to believe that, like our beloved computers, we all have a basic operating system—hardware that forms the basis of how we interface with the world. But there is more to it than that. We have software installed that is passed down from the generations that preceded us. Through the process of researching and writing this book, I have found my inheritance—specifically, my inherited trauma—an area of study that provides the best fit for what I have experienced in my life. Here's some of what I've learned.

* * *

Detailed in her book *Emotional Inheritance*, Dr. Galit Atlas explains how trauma can be transmitted from one generation to the next and "held in our minds and bodies as our own." This inheritance, Dr. Atlas says, is an emotional inheritance, "having a trace in our minds and in those of future generations." This new science has changed the thinking about how traumatic events are processed, by ourselves and the generations before us.

Previously, the assumption that the best way to maintain emotional stability is to erase from our minds what is unpleasant, was best distilled to a simple phrase: What you don't remember won't hurt you. However, this theory began to be challenged after World War II, when psychoanalysts first began examining the impact of trauma on the next generation. Many of the researchers that performed these initial studies were Jews who had escaped Europe. Their patients were Holocaust survivors themselves, and the offspring of these trauma survivors were children who carried some unconscious trace of their ancestors' pain. These studies focused on epigenetics, the non-genetic influences and modifications of gene expression. The empirical research also emphasized the major role that stress hormones play in how the brain develops and thus the biological mechanisms by which trauma is transmitted from generation to generation.

And as it turns out, I discovered that my inheritance wasn't only an epigenetic one but also a genetic one.

During the course of evaluation for a medical condition that I have had for many years, my doctors ordered an array of genetic testing to determine if there might by an inherited explanation for my symptoms. All of the tests came back negative except one: I am a carrier for the Tay-Sachs gene.

Tay-Sachs disease is a degenerative condition, meaning that symptoms become worse over time. In people with Tay-Sachs disease, the nerve cells in the brain and spinal cord are progressively destroyed, leading to paralysis. Symptoms usually first appear soon after a person is born. This condition is inherited in an autosomal recessive pattern, which means the parents of an individual with an autosomal recessive condition each carry one copy of the altered gene, but they do not show signs and symptoms of the condition. And the disease is most common in people of Ashkenazi Jewish descent—in other words, in people like me.

The nurse who relayed the results asked me an appropriate question after telling me about the results of the test: "Are you Jewish?"

"Umm . . . no . . . I mean, my father . . . his family . . . was Jewish." It was the best I could do on short notice.

We then went on to discuss the likelihood that my being a Tay-Sachs carrier had anything to do with my condition. We both agreed: not likely.

But that wasn't the point. The test result was (another) tell, a message somebody or something was trying to deliver to me about my true heritage. I was convinced of that, if nothing else.

Of course, my children need to be tested as well to see if either one is carrier which could have implications for their future children. But that issue aside, being a carrier of a disease most prevalent in Jewish people reminded me, once again, that not only have I inherited some traits that are epigenetic, like Holocaust trauma, but also at least one that is genetic.

The evidence for my Jewishness was mounting.

* * *

An important study done at the Icahn School of Medicine at Mount Sinai Hospital by Dr. Rachel Yehuda, director of the traumatic stress studies division, revealed that the offspring of Holocaust survivors have lower levels of cortisol, a hormone that helps the body recover after trauma. The research also demonstrated that the descendants of people who survived the Holocaust have different stress-hormone profiles than their peers, perhaps predisposing them to anxiety disorders. There was also an indication that healthy offspring of Holocaust survivors, as well as of enslaved people and war veterans, who experienced major trauma are more likely to present with symptoms of PTSD after traumatic events or after witnessing a violent incident.

This concept explains a great deal about what I experienced as I got deeper and deeper into my transplant career. Organ transplantation is a magical but imperfect therapy. Some of the critically ill patients I cared for were inevitably going to die, so death was a daily companion when I went off to the hospital each day. Death was an immutable feature of what I did for a living, an aspect of the field that emerged just as prominently as did the saves—the successes that drew me into this medical specialty, where we were always navigating life and death, often in the same day in different patients, sometimes in the same hour in a specific patient.

But instead of learning to accept this as a fact of my profession—an occupational hazard, if you will—as time went on, I was incrementally traumatized by each patient that I could not save. Most of my colleagues, while dedicated, empathetic caregivers in their own right, learned to handle the losses, pick themselves up after a patient died and move onto the next one who needed their help. For a time, I could do that as well, but at the end of my run in the clinical transplant arena, I lost my ability to do so. Instead, I developed a devastating degree of distress and was ultimately diagnosed with post-traumatic stress syndrome by a therapist, a diagnosis I would not initially accept, because I felt like I hadn't "earned it" in the way some traumatized war veterans had. Whether being the son and grandson of Holocaust survivors led me to this diagnosis, I can't be sure. I was unaware at the time of the connection so I didn't mention it to my therapist. But now, the notion that what had happened to my family had an impact on me—perhaps a profound one—is not especially difficult to accept. The dots do connect.

As Dr. Atlas points out, children and grandchildren of Holocaust survivors are more vulnerable, because as she says, "The people we love and those who raised us live inside us; we experience their emotional pain. We inherit family traumas, *even those that we haven't been told about* [italics added]." That last phrase is what interested me the most: One can apparently experience all of this trauma without even being explicitly told about it, which I wasn't.

For example, she explains that the Hungarian-born psychoanalysts Mária Török and Nicolas Abraham who studied Holocaust survivors and their children in Paris "used the word 'phantom' to describe the many ways in which the second generation felt their parents' devastation and losses, even when the parents never talked about them. Their inherited feelings of the parents' unprocessed trauma were the phantoms that lived inside them."

Dr. Atlas concludes, "Everything we do not consciously know is relived. It is held in our minds and in our bodies and makes itself known to us via what we call symptoms: headaches, obsessions, phobias, insomnia can all be signs of what we have pushed away to the darkest recesses of our minds." I have struggled for many years with a chronic pain syndrome that has defied diagnostic certainty or treatment, of either a medical or psychological type. Is this persistent pain a result of my hospital experiences, superimposed on a backdrop of being the offspring of Holocaust survivors? Possibly. Association does not establish causation, as we say in medicine, but as I study this area, it does make me wonder. As Mária Török and Nicolas Abraham once wrote, "What haunts are not the dead, but the gaps left within us by the secrets of others."

In describing her own practice, Dr. Atlas makes an interesting observation: "Years later, in New York City, far from my homeland, I am surprised by how many of my patients are second and third generation descendants of Holocaust survivors. These high-functioning, successful, and productive people all have something in common: the ghosts of persecution who show themselves in unpredictable ways and at unexpected times. Under the surface they carry the trauma and guilt of the survivors. I learn that from childhood, images and daydreams of the Holocaust have been frequent visitors in their minds, even and especially for those whose parents never talked about what happened to their families during the war."

And then this from Dr. Atlas about Judaism, a faith with which I have an ever-strengthening connection as I learn about my past and consider my present: "Remembering and reenacting suffering is a part of the Jewish tradition, and it is threaded through many rituals, such as Passover Seder, where the 'memory' of slavery and liberation is relived through our senses and our actions. The reenactment of trauma links the past and the future, our history and our destiny. It turns passive victims into active agents, victims into victors." It would be hard to overstate, after reading all I could about Holocaust survivors and the emotional inheritance these victims left, how closely I identified with this passage.

* * *

What's in a name? According to Dr. Atlas's work, a great deal.

She writes that "names are a significant part of one's identity. In first sessions, I usually ask people about the meaning of their names, inquire who chose the names for them and why and wonder if there are specific meanings or stories associated with their names. Names are connected to emotions, the hopes parents have for their child, who they think the child will become or want the child to become. A name reflects the parents' feelings about having that child. It contains remembrances from the past as well as a vision of the future."

This concept resonates with me. As a child, I often asked my mother why she named me David. She always answered the same way: "David means the Beloved One." Elated with my mother's answer, I would happily run away, satisfied in some way that I was special, I was loved, a feeling that I craved then—and now. This would sustain me for a surprising length of time, and when the feeling began to fade, I would simply ask again why she named me David. And the cycle repeated.

As her book comes to its final chapter, Dr. Atlas further states that "while our journeys to healing vary, each starts with the decision *to search, to open the door, and, rather than turn away from the hurt of the past, to walk toward it* [italics added]. We choose to unpack our emotional inheritance, to be active agents in transforming our fate into destiny."

And then: "We identify with previous generations—with those who have been injured, who have been humiliated, and who have died. In our fantasy, their cure is also our own. We plead for liberation from our bonds to the painful past and from the guilt of living and having a better life than the painful past and from the guilt of living and having a better life than the people who came before us. However, that unconscious wish to heal our ancestors often prevents us from mourning everything we cannot repair, save, or start again: our own childhoods, our parents' wounds, and our grandparents."

Dr. Atlas concludes with a hopeful message, something I can carry with me as I continue on my own path toward emotional healing: "Trauma is transmitted through our minds and through our bodies, but so are resilience and healing. The next generations carry not only the despair of the past, but also hope, because their mere existence is evidence that their family survived and that a future is possible."

As Mark Wolynn asks in his book, *It Didn't Start With You,* "Would you rather be in a warzone with somebody that's had previous adversity and knows how to defend themselves? Or somebody that has never had to fight for anything?"

A good question with an obvious answer. I reminded myself not to think of past trauma as just that, trauma that caused suffering, but rather something that builds strength.

When I now think of inherited trauma, I have reconsidered the concept. Perhaps it's really inherited strength, or even inherited courage. That's what I like to think now.

If Dr. Atlas provided a background understanding of emotional inheritance, what else can be discovered about the legacy of the Holocaust, my legacy? What can be said more specifically about remembrance?

In a 2013 Pew Research Center survey, 73 percent of American Jews said that remembering the Holocaust was "essential to being

Jewish"—more than those who said the same of "working for justice/equality" or "caring about Israel." But the form that Holocaust remembrance takes has never been more urgent. The youngest Holocaust survivors with any memory of the experience are pushing ninety.

The first generation—the survivors themselves as well as those trying to tell survivors' stories in the first couple of decades after the Holocaust—were understandably obsessed with transmitting the facts. Elie Wiesel's *Night* and Primo Levi's *If This Is a Man* (also known as *Survival in Auschwitz*) are books about their authors' experiences. And one can assume Anne Frank intended that a version of her diary would function as a testimony.

The second generation—the children of survivors—wrestled with their ambivalent relationship to the event, which was proximate enough to affect them enormously. "If a chasm opened in the lives of the First Generation, they could nonetheless sigh on the far side and recall the life Before," the novelist Melvin Jules Bukiet, the son of a survivor, wrote in 2001, "but for the Second Generation there is no Before. In the beginning was Auschwitz."

In contrast, the third generation is far enough removed not to possess such intimate legacies. In place of the first generation's unassailable credibility, the second generation's anguish is the third generation's aloofness and modesty. The third generation has also benefited from a wildly different information environment, owing to the continued national fascination with the Holocaust—piqued by the trial of Adolf Eichmann in 1961, magnified by the much-watched 1978 NBC mini-series *Holocaust*, and turbocharged in 1993 by *Schindler's List* and the opening of the US Holocaust Memorial Museum in Washington.

According to my understanding, I could be considered either a second- or third-generation survivor. Others, less comfortable with the term *survivor,* prefer to be called children or grandchildren of Holocaust survivors, or descendants of survivors. My grandfather was in a concentration camp so he was definitely a first-generation survivor. My father was uprooted from his native country, his young life turned upside down by the events in Germany. Was my father a first generation survivor or a second? And therefore, was I a second- or third-generation survivor? I could argue it either way, but it may not be important to make a distinction. The Holocaust profoundly affected my family, so it has profoundly affected me.

Regardless of what definition one chooses, this passage by Amy Kurzweil in her memoir *Flying Couch* describes well the role the Holocaust played for people like me: "To be of the third generation, its members insist, is to have just the right proximity to the event—close enough to want to keep it in memory, not so close to want it in the present tense; close enough to think it is a part of them, not so close to think it cannot have different meanings for others. The Holocaust is one of our most well-documented historical atrocities in the West, there's a kind of obsession with it—but there's something weird about being personally, in your family, connected to this history they make Hollywood movies about, because then you start to see your history as a Hollywood movie." Then she cautions, "You don't want to fall into self-mythologizing," she added. "It's a confusing inheritance."

In many areas that I study, whether it's a new research finding in medicine or the revelations discovered while working on this book, my natural tendency is to ask the question: *So what?* In other words, *Why does it all matter? What's the rub?* The same is true of the concept of inherited trauma. Yes, it's quite possible that I have experienced it, mostly unwittingly, but I'm married to it nonetheless. And how did it manifest in me?

Perfectionism—a character trait that has led to accomplishments of which I am proud and failures of which I'm not. Striving for perfection resulted in a successful career and other accomplishments that I achieved in a (mostly) functional way.

One might reasonably ask, *What does perfectionism have to do with inherited trauma or the search for religious identity?* Plenty, as it turns out.

In *The Perfection Trap: Embracing the Power of Good Enough,* Thomas Curran wrote that "perfectionists tend to deal with anxiety by overthinking. We suppose that covering every possible base is the most fail-safe method of holding things together, forgetting that overthinking is itself a handicapping form of anxiety." Many of us do this in spite of the observation by psychologist Asher Pacht that "true perfection exists only in obituaries and eulogies."

In my case, I'm certain that the pursuit of perfection—and the things that pursuit achieved—was a way to tell myself that *I'm enough.* It was akin to the feeling I got when I was told I was a handsome little boy (*aren't all young boys told this?*), picked first for sports teams when I was younger, when a transplant patient of mine told me that I had saved her life, or when my patients' families would stand and clap as I walked past them in the waiting room on my way to the ICU.

Gratitude, affirmation. *Tell Me I'm Enough. Tell Me I Belong.* It has been the reason I get out of bed in the morning, I realize now. But there's a flip side, as Curran points out: "On the rare occasion that it's mentioned in diagnostic criteria, it (perfectionism) tends to be one of many symptoms associated with obsessive-compulsive disorder (OCD). It's an entire worldview." In other words, people like me are putting ourselves through the wringer for validation, for the feeling from other people that we're worth something in the world. Chasing perfection, and in some cases achieving it, "relieves shame-based fears of not being good enough to matter, or be loved by other people, which is the same thing."

But here is the reality about perfectionism: "It's an exhausting way of going through life, needing to be perfect, correcting or concealing what's imperfect," Paul Hewitt said in Curran's *The Perfection Trap*. "And that leaves absolutely no room for respite or compassionate self-reflection." As much as I would like to blame my pursuit of perfection on someone else—work colleagues, friends, family, even competitors (imagined or real)—mine was inherited, passed down to me from all that came before me. And I helped it flourish, continuing the trend set by my ancestors. I know that now, and I'm determined to let this character trait end with me and not show up in my daughters.

PART FOUR

MEANING: THE LAST PART

Once you really know yourself, can't nobody tell you nothing about you.

—*Megan Thee Stallion*

The author at his desk, 2024

CHAPTER ONE

DAVID WEILL (ME)

New Orleans, 1964–Present

As I wrote this book—and of course, performed the research and wallowed in contemplation and rumination—my thoughts continually drifted back to my own nuclear family, even as I dwelled on the experiences of my ancestors. I imagined all of it like a photograph, the old kind, a printed-out Polaroid with tattered edges, my daughters and wife in the foreground, in sharp focus, my ancestors, hundreds, if not thousands, in the background, blurry but visible.

I knew that I couldn't do much about what my ancestors went through—both the good and the bad—their history was theirs, already baked in. But what my children would experience, how my two daughters might interpret the world, I could have a hand in that or, at the very least, be around to witness it, in moments just like this.

* * *

When we moved to New Orleans from California in 2016, my oldest daughter, Hannah, was entering high school and Ava was starting middle school. Although I was familiar with the social construct of my hometown, my children were not, so there was a bit of a recalibration period for them. Part of that adjustment revolved around the debutante and Mardi Gras scenes—two social activities that seem intertwined because the same multigenerational families are involved with both. Growing up there, mine was not one of those families. I had many friends who were quite involved in both, though—decent people mostly, but with a different legacy than mine. On balance, I was happy not to participate in either: the fancy balls, the countless nights in a tuxedo, the focus on birthright as if it were achievement, and the self-congratulation that came with being part of the "right" family. But my kids didn't understand all of this, so at times, I had to do some explaining. I welcomed the opportunity. It's always revealing for your children when they first discover something that you have known for years—a glimpse into a parent's lived experience that makes them look at the parent in a new way.

"Will Ellie Goldstein have a deb party?" Hannah asked, as we sat at our kitchen table one Saturday morning. She was referring to a high school classmate who was now of debutante age.

"No. The Goldsteins are Jewish," I said. She gave me an Instagram-honed WTF look. It didn't compute for her.

"Jewish?"

"Yeah, you know, Jewish. Synagogues, Hanukkah, et cetera. The whole bit." She didn't flinch, accustomed to my commentary, which could be snarky at times.

"Will the Sorkins have a deb party then?" She was referring to another Jewish family whose daughter had attended high school with her, a family with multigenerational roots in New Orleans.

"No. Jew." I decided to use shorthand for this part of the NOLA lesson.

Hannah sat there for a moment, looking away and then back at me. "That's fucked up." We use salty language in our family.

"Yes, but that's our town, sweetie. Take the good with the bad." I went back to my newspaper.

Hannah just nodded, processing a New Orleans fact of life, or maybe just a fact of life, that was archaic and hard to understand. But I hoped it was not something she would dwell on, not like I had over the years. Her religious identity was more clear cut—Catholic at birth. She'll quite likely be Catholic when she dies. There has been no indication that she has given her religion a second thought and that is a blessing, for which I am thankful.

But for me, on the other hand, there was more work to do.

As all study and consideration of my family's experience pointed me increasingly toward Judaism, I began to confront a reality that could have been an obstacle to a full embrace of the Jewish religion: I knew very little about it, not even the basics. I needed to learn even the simplest answer to the question *What is Judaism?* So, I found another book, one that delivered the information I needed in an easily consumable manner, free of too much density or complexity.

Uncomfortable Conversations with a Jew was authored by Emmanuel Acho and Noa Tishby and, it seems, written especially for me. In a question-and-answer format between Acho and Tishby, subjects relating to Judaism were explored in an easily digestible format. In fact, many of the questions posed in the book were exactly the questions I had, such as simple ones like *Who (or What) on Earth is a Jew?*

Tishby provided straightforward answers to questions like this, such as Judaism is "not just a religion, it's an ethno-religion—meaning being Jewish is not solely about being observant or practicing daily rituals. It's about a shared story and history, a shared culture . . ." Apparently, being Jewish does not necessarily mean adherence to a specific set of tenets, or a belief in the afterlife, or anything else. It's about being part of a peoplehood. It's about belonging. And that's what I was looking for. Jews are not interested in being told what they should, or should not, believe, but instead seek a recognition of who they belong to, who are their/my people. To me, this all made sense.

Some of the other questions that were posed and answered by the authors made sense to me too, such as: *How do you Jew?* This more than slightly tongue-in-cheek question was answered in a simple way: however you want to. Devout practitioner or a part-timer for the High Holidays, it all worked. It was all okay. The flexibility greatly appealed to me, especially after being a practicing Catholic for over a decade. Of all the strong attributes associated with Catholicism, flexibility is not one of them. And yes, I can hear what a Catholic priest might say: The rituals *are* the religion, the doctrines immutable—not like a Chinese menu where a practitioner could pick and choose their favorite beliefs and all was good. No, Catholicism doesn't work that way, and there may be valid reasons why that is so, but let me go on the record and say this: I don't love the rigidity of the Catholic Church. It's not my favorite part and not reflective of how I conduct the rest of my life, where the status quo is continually questioned and, at times, railed against.

There was more.

In a section titled "So, What Is Judaism?" Tishby distills the essence of the religion into a few basic tenets. Judaism is a decentralized religion that emphasizes community, celebrates nature, evolves as we do, and is a big tent. I believe in all of that. Tishby relates how a friend of hers, Gidi Grinstein, looks at Judaism. Grinstein believes that Judaism can be viewed through four pillars: religion, peoplehood, *tikkun alam*, and nationhood. Tishby says that "religion and faith are personal and are observed differently by different individuals. Peoplehood can be described as shared stories: legacy, history, family, and educational tradition, which link many generations. *Tikkun alam* is the Jewish mandate to make the world a better place, literally to 'mend it.' And nationhood is the modern manifestation of a basic human need: a connection to a land and the need for self-determination and self-governance. Not every Jew practices or identifies with all four pillars, but I think they are a great prism to use when thinking about one's Jewishness."

Amen. I love that. It works for me.

But what about the culture? I mean, how often have I heard someone say, *I don't really practice Judaism. I'm a cultural Jew.*

What does that really mean? Is there some place that one gets sent to for special training?

Well, Tishby answers this question as well in a section of the book titled "The Culture Club," a section that could have just as easily been titled the "The Tribal Club." She says that aside from having the "compulsive need to feed" people, the culture of being Jewish also means having an interest in storytelling—at holidays, over a meal—just about any time. Some of the stories are repetitious, but that's okay. Repetition makes the heart grow fonder, or something like that.

There's also questioning (and arguing with) everything. Tishby says that "when something doesn't seem right, we've been instructed to question it, argue over it, and debate it until truth prevails." Or we lose the energy to do so—or all of our friends and family. It's "never being content with the status quo (or just never being content)."

I smiled when I read this. All this was beginning to remind me of my house growing up. My father led nightly dinner discussions where views were put forward and my sisters and I, even as young children, were expected to challenge them, preferably with well-considered arguments. My father was essentially coaching a junior debate team. Whether that was a good or bad thing, I have no objectivity on the matter.

Then there was education, another part of being a cultural Jew. Tishby says that "the directive to read and write is woven into Judaism." That's certainly how I was raised, with a mother who was an avid reader, constantly handing her children books to read—novels, works of nonfiction, anything. My father was an academic writer of unparalleled precision, with a superb command of the English language, which is often the case with immigrants who make words a primary obsession.

Finally, the last part of being a cultural Jew, the valuing of the here and now. According to Tishby, one finds "very few mentions of the afterlife in the Hebrew Bible." Rabbi Jonathan Sacks says, "Judaism is an extraordinarily this-worldly, this-life-focused religion." I reread this sentence a few times. *How different from Catholicism*, I thought, which focuses so much on the afterlife that, at times, a leap of faith is necessary to practice the religion—which may be exactly what is required to be a true believer.

* * *

All of the reading and new insight I was gaining was nourishing the intellectual part of me, but sometimes the heart and the gut take over, and the mind recedes into the background. Events supersede everything and the books are put to the side, at least for a time. October 2023 presented just one of those moments.

Gaza protest site at Tulane University, New Orleans, 2024

CHAPTER TWO

NEW ORLEANS

October 7, 2023

AT THE BEGINNING OF THIS BOOK, I WROTE ABOUT THE FEAR of a little boy in the wake of the attack on Israeli athletes at the 1972 Munich Games. It was my first inkling of what it means to be Jewish, even though at the time I didn't identify as such. I learned a hard lesson: Despite there being only fifteen million Jews in the world, comprising less than 0.2 percent of the world's population, there is a disproportionate amount of hate and violence directed toward this small group of people. I was too young to understand all that back then, but a more recent event put that very notion in more stark relief, deepening my understanding as I sat firmly in middle age. But my feeling of vulnerability and despondency was no different.

I sat in front of the TV and stared—quietly incredulous, then angry and tearful—the images bringing me immediately back to 9/11 and the days that followed. None of us could turn off the news back then, its horror strikingly addictive. Fast-forward to today, and a certain segment of the population—which included me—wasn't turning the TV off now either. On this October morning, most people, I suppose, went about their Saturday, going to the grocery store or yoga class, meeting someone for lunch, running errands. It wasn't their people who were being attacked. But it was my people—I felt that, finally—so I sat and watched, hand covering my mouth so I wouldn't scream out loud. The images on the television imprinted in my brain that day and nearly every day since then.

The details of the attack on Israel by Hamas began to trickle in—concertgoers gunned downed, the elderly and children kidnapped, bodies mutilated, the reports of sexual assault that made me physically ill. I have two daughters, two sisters, a wife, and a mother. How would I respond if one of these savages laid a hand on them? I didn't want to go there, not that morning, not as I stared at the television and tried to process what had happened.

In all, more than 1,200 Israelis would lose their lives. The pointlessness of it all overwhelmed me as I paced around in the comfort of my living room, the sun streaming in on a cool, bright fall morning in New Orleans. I had seen and heard similar acts of barbarism on the news recently associated with Russia's unprovoked war against Ukraine. But this felt different—my reaction was more visceral, my grief more debilitating.

Why?

Because in these images, I—a non-practicing, reluctant Jew By Definition—thought of my ancestors. The last house of worship I had entered was a Catholic church, but today, this day, I was a Jew. If the Hamas terrorists had gotten one look at me, I'd be dead, or worse. Immersed in writing this book, how could I reach any other conclusion? It is not possible to look at the heartbreaking letters my grandfather sent my grandmother from Buchenwald, to read the words written by my father and grandfather to each other years later, to absorb the plight of the Jewish people through my family's story—and then be indifferent to the fact that this attack wasn't just another display of man's inhumanity to man. This was an assault on my people, again, on my father and grandfather, on me. The difference now was simple: I was different.

As deeply disturbing as the initial reports were, the ensuing public reaction is what stung the most, especially the fecklessness of academia. All of it was appalling—the ill-informed student protesters, the lack of moral compass among some faculty members, the university presidents who couldn't quite answer the question. I watched the congressional hearings of these people—those who had climbed to the top of the academic ladder—and watched them dance around the question, a simple one really: *Would you condemn Jewish hate speech on your campus?* Then more dancing, more calculation in their heads about how to respond, about what would play in the faculty lounge. All I could do was scream at the TV screen: *Answer the fucking question! The question, idiot.*

I had spent the vast majority of my career in an academic environment, so I had seen it up close. In watching all this, the saddest part for me was how unsurprised I was by what was happening on our college campuses. For a community that is so concerned with "appropriate" language, so protective of pronouns, so fervently self-righteous, the lack of moral compass was astonishing, the unwillingness or inability to make a clear-eyed assessment of what had just happened astounding. The cognitive dissonance rampant in certain sectors of academia and the contradictions and moral equivalency was startling—and all this before one IDF plane was in the air, before one brigade of ground troops was deployed. I had seen many forms of demonstrations on college campuses during my time as a student and faculty member—protests against apartheid in South Africa, the Trump-era Muslim travel bans, and the outrage following the murder of George Floyd. I had walked by these protests, often nodding or giving a quick fist pump. But this time was different. I didn't want to just walk by, to keep my views to myself. I wanted to talk with one of the protesters.

Our family lives near the Tulane University campus, a lovely college setting that fronts Audubon Park. The park has a beautiful circular walking path that is surrounded by oak trees and small lagoons filled with South Louisiana critters of all types. I walk my two dogs in the park every morning, a forty-five-minute jaunt that I relish. It is a time for reflection and serenity, the latter of which my brain doesn't allow as much as I'd like. But there was something that cropped up and took my serenity away and stole my peace.

Soon after October 7, anti-Israeli protests began—with tents and signs and chants spewing the usual slogans. For the first few weeks, I just eyed the protesters and largely tried to ignore them, not wanting to disrupt the best part of my day. But after watching all this for a month or so, and hearing the stupidity coming from the bullhorns as the sun was just beginning to rise, I decided to engage. "C'mon," I said to the dogs.

"From the river to the sea," the young man with shaggy blond hair shouted. He was the leader of the group, and his followers had just emerged from their tents, looking like they were in need of a cup of coffee and a shower. I had a look around. Fast-food bags littered the front lawn of the campus. *This would be a movement fueled by Uber Eats*, I thought to myself. Every shouted slogan was then repeated in unison by the fifty or so bleary-eyed students who had emerged from their sleeping bags. As is their wont, most of the students had their phones out, taking video of the proceedings. With this generation, if images aren't recorded and posted on social media—whether it's a picture of their lunch or a new outfit, or calls to end "Zionist genocide"—then none of it really happened.

I stood and watched, my dogs sitting quietly, taking in the scene with me. After several minutes, the blond kid stopped shouting, took a sip from his Starbucks cup, and accepted a few high fives from his followers.

Then, I walked over. "Hey," I said. He turned to me, and we stood face to face. I'm sure he viewed me as nonthreatening, as one would when confronted by a middle-aged man with two labradoodles and pockets overflowing with poop bags. He nodded to me, with a hint of a scowl that I thought was intended to limit conversation. "Can I ask you a question?"

He kept a neutral expression of his face, likely interpreting the question as a rhetorical one, which it was.

I started in. "Are you conflicted at all, by what you're doing here, with what happened on October 7? It was some pretty awful shit." I tried to communicate as best I could in a way that he might understand.

"No, I'm not . . ."

"Oh, you're not?" I felt the blood rush to my face, an early warning system that I recognized—a prelude, usually, to language and behavior that don't reveal my best self.

"No, I'm not. October 7 was a justified attack, given the policies of the Israeli government toward the Palestinians." The kid nodded to himself, dead certain of his silly assertion.

"So terrorism is okay if it serves a certain policy objective."

He blinked a few times. A car went by with unrolled windows.

The driver honked and shouted, "Idiots." The guy in the car perhaps thought I was one of the protesters.

I continued. "So 9/11 was okay because Bin Laden's people had a legitimate beef with the US?"

"Well . . ."

I cut him off. "And January 6 was okay because the election didn't go the way the people who invaded the capital wanted it to go?"

"Look, dude, those were different. This is genocide, man."

That did it. "I don't need a lecture on genocide. The people I come from"—I could feel a vein popping out of my forehead—"they saw genocide up close." Then I nodded toward the campus buildings. "I know they teach students about the Holocaust here, because I studied it—a long time ago."

"The United Nations, everyone thinks this is genocide."

I rolled my eyes. "The United Nations . . ."

"You must not believe in free speech," he said.

That made me laugh. "Oh, I do. I'm not sure some in your generation believe in it, though. How many speakers get disinvited from colleges every day because it doesn't conform with the dogma?"

"You don't get it," he said, a go-to line of the intellectually lazy.

"Oh, I do, my friend." My dogs sat up and pulled on their leashes. Apparently Lucy and Frannie had heard enough—and so had I.

I started to walk away, to do the mature thing befitting my sixty years on the planet, but ultimately, I couldn't help myself. I turned around and asked the guy, who was watching me walk away, "By the way, what river is it? What sea?" It was not an original response on my part, one I learned from the op-ed columnists of various outlets, but nonetheless, it was the best I could do on short notice. After all, my intention that morning was to simply walk my dogs, not to engage some ill-informed college student.

“Fuck you, man,” he said without changing expression, appearing neither attacked by my comment nor outraged in any way.

“Thought so,” I said and left it at that. All this before my morning cup of coffee.

On my walk back home, I stood up straighter, my gait steady and assured, my mind more settled.

What I heard from the protester was acceptable free speech in 2024, the rationalization of terror, the aspiration to push a country into the sea for the crime of defending itself. As I made the short walk back home—a man with his two dogs—I felt centuries of Weill Family rabbis with me. I thought of Kippenheim. I thought of Buchenwald. I thought of my father when the knock came on the door, the Nazis showing up to take my grandfather away, his early life on the run because society—not all of it, but substantial parts of it—had decided that Jews should be killed, that it was tolerable, even warranted. And it seemed some important parts of society had now decided the same thing again—Islamic extremists (unsurprisingly), but also Western European governments (somewhat surprisingly), and some college campuses (surprising only at first thought, but not at second and third thoughts).

Family farm of Jackie Weill, Rockwell, Iowa, 2024

CHAPTER THREE

IOWA

April 2024

I WAS ON A VIDEO CONFERENCE CALL WHEN MY PHONE buzzed. It was Jackie.

I pressed the button to send the call to voicemail. While I am almost always available by phone (sadly), Jackie knows that when I don't pick up I'm either swimming laps or in a meeting. Otherwise, I pick up. Day or night—an occupational habit I formed during my decades taking organ donor calls on the transplant service.

Then she texted. *Call me. My mother had a stroke.*

I looked at my computer screen, the green light of the video camera staring back at me. I heard voices from my computer, distant now, in the background of something far more important that was now front and center. *We'd like you to plan a visit to the hospital, to meet with the transplant team to discuss . . .*

I wasn't paying attention.

"Can we finish up by email? I . . . I have to go . . ." I said, hastily leaving the virtual meeting.

I dialed my wife's number and went into doctor mode, my first—but not always my best—instinct.

"Is she moving? Talking? How long was she down?"

Then I shut myself up. *Be a husband, not a doctor.*

"Jackie . . . I'm so sorry." Then: "Let's get you up there."

Jackie arrived in Iowa just in time. The doctor in charge debriefed the family, giving them the same grim recap that he had given me on the phone while Jackie was en route. He had spoken like I often did in these situations, in sentence fragments that didn't need a subject or verb, or anything else. *Brain aneurysm. CT scan with ventricular shift. Vitals unstable,* he said, as I took down the information on a sticky note, just as I had so many times before when a nurse or one of my colleagues told me about one of my own patients.

Then I asked/stated as a matter of fact: "Then . . . no chance of meaningful recovery?" The only question worth asking at that point. "So I can talk to the family . . ." I said, but I needed to know, also.

"No," the doctor replied, without any hedge or hint of uncertainty. When a doctor doesn't cloak bad news in either caveats or conditional responses, take it to heart. That was it. There was nothing left to say.

Now it was time to be a husband, a father to my daughters who just lost their grandmother, and a grieving son-in-law—and it was time to prepare for a funeral.

I flew with Ava to Minneapolis where we would meet Hannah, who was flying in from North Carolina. When Hannah met us at our arrival gate, we hugged, the three of us holding each other tightly.

During the two-hour drive to my wife's hometown in northern Iowa, my daughters and I talked about their grandmother, the memories we all had, and the pain that Jackie was experiencing. We also talked about death—how sudden it can be, an unexpected visitor that sometimes doesn't announce itself, instead just showing up at a moment's notice. My daughters had mostly experienced the slow kind of death—my father's, most notably—where there was time to prepare oneself, to adjust to a new reality that was in clear sight.

I then turned to a subject that was more difficult for them, but one I thought we had to broach to take advantage of a teachable moment that might not present itself anytime soon.

"Girls, my time will come someday, so will Mom's—and so will yours." Young people who are healthy never think that's true. I mostly took care of patients who had chronic diseases their whole life. They knew. But young people like my kids, not so much. I was grateful for that.

I looked in the rearview mirror at Ava, who looked up from her phone. "I guess so, Dad, then it will be time for heaven."

"Yep. And they'll all be there—my father, Lexi and Roxy (our dogs who had passed), and now grandma." I nodded, to help convince myself that was true as the conversation moved to lighter topics—both kids' graduations, summer plans, and what their friends were doing. Then we settled back into the drive, the passing corn fields, the gently rolling landscape that in spring was just starting to turn from brown to green. We drove along in silence, listening to one of my daughters' playlists, each of us absorbed in our own thoughts. I only wondered what would await us when we arrived at the funeral home.

* * *

Envy can be part of any relationship, including marriage—but the emotion need not be a negative one. Rather than a manifestation of insecurities or petty jealousies, one can be envious of their spouse because some of their traits are the subject of longing and desire—in effect saying, *I wish I had that,* or *I wish I was that.* One can be envious of excellent health, good sleep habits, or how someone remains serene in the company of the annoying. I felt all of those things when it came to Jackie, but all these petty jealousies paled in comparison to the granddaddy of them all: her faith. That one I wanted, not just since we were married on a hot August day in Dallas in 1998, but every day since then. She had it, and I wanted it.

Her faith was on full display at the funeral home.

When my daughters and I walked in, family and friends were milling about, quietly talking among themselves, exchanging handshakes and hugs. A Catholic priest, a tall man with red hair, stood at the front of the room, hands folded in front of him, nodding as his parishioners walked by. There was one startling presence, though: Janet, Jackie's mother, lying in an open casket. I took one glance, and as someone who had seen his fair share of dead people at work, I still couldn't fix my gaze on Janet's motionless body. It was too much. I didn't have an especially close relationship with my mother-in-law, but this? No. I needed to avoid *this.*

But as I looked at Jackie, even in the presence of her recently deceased mother, her expression never changed. She was sad, yes, but in some way, accepting. How could this be?

It took her mother's death, and more specifically her reaction to it—her actions and attitude about it, from the first hours after we heard the terrible news to this day—for me to really understand what true faith looked like. It was unambiguous, innate, a central aspect of one's soul that isn't influenced by life circumstances, whims, or intellectualism. Faith is higher than that, a principle that stands above other more mundane concerns.

I didn't have that, not yet. My view toward religion and spirituality lived in my mind, something that could be manipulated by rational thought. It didn't live in my heart, a natural residence for things of this sort. I couldn't help but contrast what I saw from Jackie with my own reaction to my father's death, an inevitable passing after a long series of health concerns, so different from the suddenness of Janet's death. I would never have what she had, not as long as I didn't find my true religious identity, instead of co-opting hers, no matter how well intentioned.

I realized this that day at the funeral home—an unexpected collateral emotion to the passing of a kind and dear woman. But that's what it took.

The next day was the church service. Jackie asked me to be a pallbearer, so I stood outside the church with a group of men that I didn't know, distant relatives of Jackie that I had never met. We made small talk about the weather, the prospects of the Iowa Hawkeye football team, even the traffic that slowly crept by the street in front of the church. Anything but the task at hand.

The hearse arrived and we got the casket to the right place. That mission accomplished, I took a seat in the second row of the church pews, next to my daughters and directly behind my wife and father-in-law, Tom. Members of the community filed in behind us, a hundred or more in all, sturdy men and women in their nicest clothes, mostly farm people who were well-dressed for this day out of respect.

As I sat there, eyes closed, I heard the words from the priest about death being a "transition" to something better, into the warmth of God's love. The words got me thinking even more about my own religious beliefs. I had already questioned, quietly, in the recesses of my own mind, my Catholic faith. My religious affiliation was adopted later in life, and I admit, it mostly felt that way. I didn't share these thoughts, not at the time anyway—not with my wife, not with anyone. I was still sorting. But my longing to find my Jewish faith, to adopt it as my own, finally, was awake in me. I wondered if I should try to store it in a closet, lock it away, treat it as just another annoyance in a lifetime of ambivalence about religion. Or should I embrace it? That was what was on my mind as the Priest spoke, my mother-in-law's casket nearby.

I looked at my daughters and then at my grieving wife sitting in the pew in front of me. Her family's Catholicism was theirs. I had borrowed it in a time of trouble and it's not an overstatement to say it saved me. I won't forget that, not ever.

This church service, pallbearer, Iowa, Jackie's family. I looked around wondering if this would be my last significant interaction with Catholicism.

Then the priest interrupted my mind swirl: "Our relationship with Janet has not ended, it's just changed." Everyone nodded. I went back into my head, hearing and even saying fragments of the Lord's Prayer, *Thy will be done, on earth as it is in heaven . . . For the kingdom, the power, and the glory are yours now and forever.* My eyes were closed as I said, *Amen.*

The priest then continued: "Our sister in faith is now at home in God's kingdom. Her loved ones will rejoin her one day." Jackie turned to smile at her father, sister, and brothers. It was a warm smile, one that said, *I got you.*

Who said religion serves no purpose? Whoever does must have not been in the church that day, or any place like it.

Then, finally, my favorite part of any Mass, when you shake hands with strangers and hug and kiss your own family, and say, *Peace be with you.* And you mean it. It is warm, it is comforting, and for that moment, this religion, or just religion, makes so much sense to me.

I watched Jackie some more, I couldn't keep my eyes off her. She closed her eyes as the priest spoke. Her grief was so apparent, written on a face that I knew every twitch of after a quarter century of marriage. If her grief was obvious to me, so was the comfort she was feeling in this church, on full display as she sat next to her father.

In that moment, I have never admired her more. We had our ups and downs, a marriage that at times met neither of our expectations, but when I think of her, in good times and bad, I think of her faith, her character. She is rooted in it—and it may be her defining feature, providing a foundation through which she takes care of her family, the bedrock of her sturdiness in that church on that day. I wanted what she had; I wanted it all along, including when I chose to become Catholic, but I couldn't have it. I wanted it, but it wasn't mine.

My people were German Jews, in every way, even though the Great Dispersion had scattered them. My people were more likely to be in New York or Los Angeles, not in the rural Midwest, not anywhere near a farm. At the risk of being braggadocious, my family, I had come to learn, was German aristocracy—in terms of wealth, yes, but also in the arts, scholarship, and rabbinical studies. We were a family that was part of the intellectual bourgeoisie. We were, that is, until we were on trains to other countries, boats to other continents, or, for the unlucky ones, on transport to death camps in the East. That was my family. Those were my people.

Lights off in our hotel room, restless in bed, the last thing I heard that night was my daughters talking and laughing in the adjoining room. It had been a long day, but these were the most beautiful sounds of my life, a symphony on full display in that dark room in rural Iowa. The howling winds shook the windows and the nearby cornfields, only a few blocks from the chain hotel by the highway. I marveled at how lucky I was, not to be alone, to be trusted and supported by my family, my triumphs and tribulations theirs, and theirs mine. I shed the millionth tear of the day as I drifted off to sleep.

I was transitioning, not in the profound way that my mother-in-law had, but in my own way, in my own sphere. Regardless, I felt God's love that night, more than I ever had.

The next day before my daughters and I started the two-hour drive to the airport, we went back out of town to the farm to say goodbye to Jackie's father. While I waited for Jackie to finish getting ready, I sat on the back porch with Hannah in absolute silence and looked out at the vast farmland that stretched all the way to the horizon. There was not a living creature, not a building, not a car in my sight-line, just gently rolling cornfields and then more cornfields. But the light from the rising sun spread out across the land in a way I had never seen before, as if the light was gently touching the ground, barely making contact. I had been to Iowa dozens of times in the past but had never taken note of its beauty before, not in this way. I had never bothered to. But that day, I finally understood where my wife came from, who she was, after twenty-five years of marriage. And maybe during this trip, brought about by the most devastating of circumstances, I finally figured out where I came from.

The wind was still blowing when we got in the car to head back to the Minneapolis airport. It hadn't stopped for two days, not for a minute.

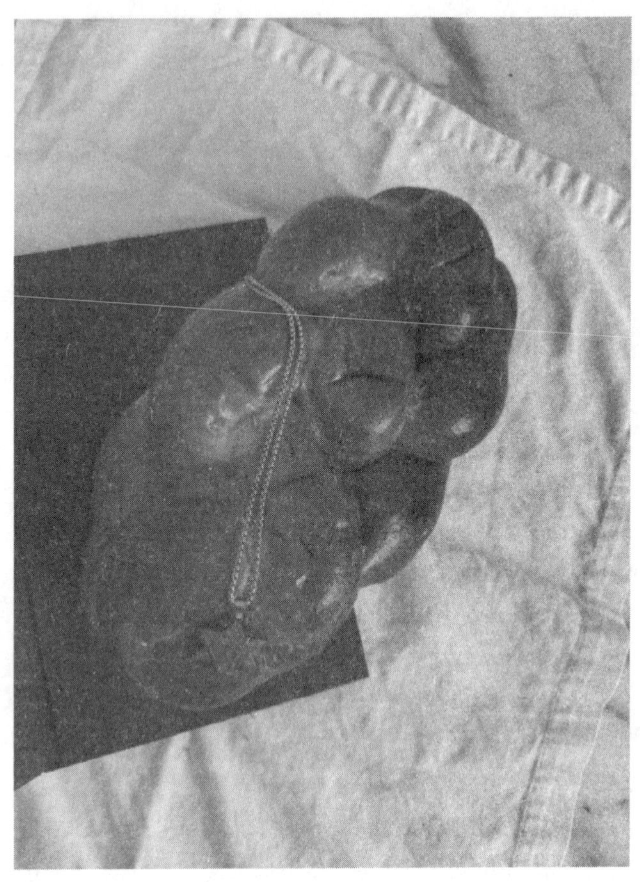

Challah bread at a Shabbat dinner, New Orleans, 2025

CHAPTER FOUR

HERE ALL ALONG

Alys Beach, Florida, June 2024

On a breezy, warm morning, I settled into a chair on the front porch and looked out to the Gulf of Mexico. The crash of the surf in the background was comforting, one of my favorite sounds of all, right up there with the laughter of my daughters. Young children walked by our house, admonishing their parents to hurry up as they got closer to the beach. I'd go down to the water's edge later, a place where I did my best thinking, my best living.

But for now I had something else on my mind: my relationship to Judaism. And the guidance provided by Sarah Hurwitz's insightful book *Here All Along: Finding Meaning, Spirituality, and a Deeper Connection to Life—In Judaism.*

As I began the book, I nodded as I read one of the early passages in the preface: "When you have a name like Sarah Hurwitz, people assume you know what you're doing in Jewish settings, and I was too ashamed of my ignorance to admit otherwise." *Try having a name like David Weill, Sarah.* I smiled to myself. I was going to like this book.

What was I hoping to learn from Sarah's book? Really just one thing: What is this Jewish thing, being a Jew, you know?

I didn't have to wait long for, at least, Hurwitz's answer to this question: "This is what Judaism is—it's not just a religion, it is the story of a large, diverse family. If you're a Christian, but you one day decide that Jesus Christ was not the son of God and did not die for your sins, and that you don't believe in God at all, you may well conclude that you're no longer a Christian. By contrast, being Jewish, as the Israeli academic Ze'ev Maghen puts it, 'is a lot more like being one of the Goldblatt kids.'"

Hurwitz continues, "No matter how estranged you are from your family, no matter how vehemently you reject their values, no matter whether you change your name and join another family, there is nothing you can do to erase the fact of being your parents' offspring. It's the same with being Jewish: If you're Jewish, even if you disavow every single Jewish belief and convert to some other religion, Jewish law still considers you to be Jewish. You are always part of this family and its story. It is your story too."

It *is* my story, I thought, this story, the one I've told on these pages. This religion is mine, I think it is, anyway, even if there is less formality to it. It seemed, at least to me, that the core of the Jewish religion is an engagement with ethics and rituals known as *Halakha*, which means "the way of walking." Judaism focuses on behavior, not necessarily faith, with the key question asking not "What may I believe?" but rather "What shall I do next?" I liked that and couldn't help but compare this approach to that of Catholicism, my adopted religion. I was beginning to discover that there are many ways to be Jewish, to claim Judaism as one's own.

So *is* this my identity? This is what Hurwitz says: "By identifying as a 'cultural Jew,' I really meant that I felt like I had a 'Jewish personality'; funny in an edgy, gallows humor kind of way; anxious and convinced the worst is always going to happen; intellectual and into arguing about ideas." I had some of these traits—perhaps, not all of them, but some of them. No one who knows me would say otherwise. But is a certain personality, or a certain culture, all that is required in order to claim Judaism? Turns out that for many people, it is.

A 2013 study by the Pew Research Center found that while 94 percent of American Jews feel proud to be Jewish, 22 percent of them, including 32 percent of Jewish millennials, "describe themselves as having no religion and identify as Jewish on the basis of ancestry, ethnicity, or culture." A full two-thirds of these Jews of no religion report that they're not raising their kids with any kind of Jewish identity.

But this doesn't mean that Jews have a natural tendency to identify with other religions. Hurwitz writes that "even some of the most disaffected Jews will admit that something inside them feels unsettled. Even if they won't go anywhere near a synagogue, it still doesn't feel quite right to attend their partners' churches on Easter or have Christmas trees in their living rooms. That still tugs at them." *Yes, it does.* In fact, Hurwitz writes, "There is a Yiddish phrase for this: *dos pintele yid,* which literally means 'that little point of a Jew' and refers to that spark of Jewishness in each of us that we can't quite manage to ignore, no matter how hard we may try." And boy, how I have tried. I guess I'm not the only one who is confused, given that there is a Yiddish phrase for this disposition.

I felt reassured by what Hurwitz wrote, taking a sip from my coffee cup, closing my eyes against the warmth of the sun rising higher over the beach. I was starting to get it.

All of what I read so far spoke to a disposition toward Judaism, a way to view the religion, say, from an observation deck, detached from the specifics of its worship. I needed more detail, more about what Jews believe, the same kind of thing I wanted to discover when I learned about Catholicism.

However, as it turns out, the Jewish faith is a bit more nebulous than Catholicism—or even Christianity—less rigid, less proscriptive, more flexible. I admit that I am attracted to this. Apparently, something I did not know about Judaism, there is no universally accepted creed or article of faith defining the Divine. I found that astonishing, and perhaps a bit liberating, since, in a massive understatement, Catholicism teaches otherwise.

Further to this point, Hurwitz writes that "I hope it's now clear that if you're simply looking for rules to memorize or dogma to unthinkingly accept, you should look elsewhere. If you're a dictator looking for a religion to be, as Karl Marx once put it, the 'opium of the people,' I would not recommend Judaism. No wonder fundamentalists and fascists have hated it so."

Instead, Hurwitz suggests to those contemplating, or re-contemplating, Judaism, to "embrace the nuance and complexity." Nuance and complexity. These are two of my favorite things. Without both of them, who would I be? What would I fixate on? This Jewish thing might be a perfect fit for me.

And, it seems, obsessing over belief in God is not a feature of Judaism, as far as I can tell. Hurwitz points out that "Judaism's primary concern is not how strongly we *believe*, but how we *behave*—not just what we *think and feel*, but what we actually do." So to the question "Are you a believer?" Hurwitz suggests that "in Judaism, that's just not the question. When other Jews are trying to suss out how religious I am, they want to know whether I keep kosher, observe Shabbat, am I a member of a synagogue. These are questions about what I *do*, not what I *believe*."

I thought about the question *What do I do?* rather than *What do I believe?* I had been conditioned when thinking about religion to think about *What do I believe?* Are my beliefs consistent, in compliance with whatever the teachings of a particular religion are? Instead, in Judaism, the "what I do" part seems paramount: keeping kosher, observing Shabbat, attending services at a synagogue.

I wanted to see the *What do I do?* up close, so I got myself invited to my book editor's home for Shabbat dinner while I was visiting New York.

"I'm nervous," I told Claire Wachtel on the Thursday afternoon before I was scheduled to go over to her apartment on the Upper West Side. Over the course of working on my first two books, and now a third, Claire and I had developed a relationship that went far beyond author and editor. She helped me with my writing, trying her best to transform a doctor-writer into a writer-doctor. I suppose I lent her some assistance when medical issues came up, but there was more to it than that, a relationship that wasn't simply transactional. Ours was a true friendship that included deep discussions on a wide range of topics that were of mutual interest—politics, culture, society, and, yes, religion.

"Nervous? About what?" Claire asked.

"I don't know, all of it." I paced around my hotel room in Midtown, the phone plastered to my ear. Then I thought, *Why am I nervous? What were they going to do? Give me some kind of Judaism test? Well . . . maybe,* I thought, irrationally. "I don't know anything about it, the prayers, the ritual, the food."

"The food?" This got a laugh out of Claire. "Did you forget how to eat?"

"Just don't ask me to do anything, to say anything."

"So you'll sit there mute?" This is why I am so fond of Claire, in moments just like this. Aside from my father, no one has ever spoken to me this bluntly, and he was long gone. I missed the directness, in a world that so often talks around matters both big and small.

"You know what I mean. Think of me as an outside observer. Like one of those people at the United Nations, wearing the little translation headphones."

"Don't worry about it. My daughter, husband, and another couple will be there. All nice people. You'll be fine."

"I hope there's wine." I pressed my hand against the window, the Empire State Building in the distance, enveloped by dark, gray clouds. "Is that allowed?"

"It's allowed."

"Thank God. See you tomorrow."

The next night, Claire answered the door and led me to the dining room of her apartment. The table was beautifully set, I could see—lovely plates, candles, a couple loaves of challah wrapped in a cloth napkin.

I could smell the food cooking in the kitchen but couldn't place it. The aroma was pleasing but unfamiliar. Just then, Claire's husband, Paul, emerged from the kitchen carrying a hot dish, a potato kugel, I was told. He smiled at me and said, "Shabbat Shalom."

"Yes . . . right," I stammered. Then quickly recovered. "Shabbat Shalom." Claire smiled to herself and maybe laughed a little.

I chatted with the Wachtels' friends—a couple who lived nearby—and Claire's daughter, Rachel, who lived in Los Angeles. She and I chatted about California, the pluses and minuses as I saw it from my time there. At dinner, we talked about politics, current events, the weather. I was glad the conversation was neutral, a safe space for me to be me, just like at any other dinner party. *This was sort of a dinner party, right? Just on a Friday night with special food, maybe a prayer or two. What was the big deal?*

But was there much more to Shabbat than that? Was it just another Friday night with friends?

Put simply, according to Sarah Hurwitz, "Shabbat is a once a week enactment of a Jewish idea of the world as it should be." It's a mini-holiday, if you will, during which Jews "take a break from the exhausting display of resume virtues and enjoy a daylong celebration of eulogy virtues." Shabbat can help us connect with ourselves—and in a world in which this is rarely the case, "Everyone is fully present." I wanted some of this, I thought, as I read this part of the book. But more than that, I *needed* some of that.

Hurwitz even talks about "those occasional Shabbat dinners when I am just not in the mood . . . When I don't feel like blessing anyone. Simply, I must be there. Involuntarily, almost against my will, a better mood overtakes me." I'm in favor of that, doing things that bring meaning and happiness to one's life. Seems like a good thing.

I listened quietly, sitting perfectly still, as Paul led us through the prayer.

The night went on, conversation over matzo ball soup and roasted chicken. The discussion involved the whole table, no sidebars that are so common at dinner parties. There wasn't talk of anything Jewish, not particularly, no formality to the evening, just conversation with smart, engaging people who didn't check their phones once. I didn't either, I realized, as I said my good nights to the group. I was the first one out the door, as is my custom at evening gatherings.

My phone had stayed tucked away in my coat pocket for the entire evening, a first for me. The togetherness was enough, the engagement more than sufficient—and so vastly different from the ritual, and yes, at times rigid, customs of the Catholic Church that I had learned so much about in the last decade, that were beautiful in their own right, if completely different from what I had just witnessed. The prayers at the Wachtel Shabbat dinner evoked real emotion in me—and so did the entire evening, I thought, as I took a taxi back to my hotel, passing quickly by the brightly lit storefronts on Broadway. *This is what Jews do*, I thought. This is what they/we do. I liked it. It worked for me.

But waking up the next morning on another overcast Manhattan morning, there was still one aspect of Judaism that I needed to understand. *Just one*, you ask? Well, just one that was on my mind that morning, and many mornings before that, an occupational hazard that often leaked into my personal life: death. I needed to know where the Jewish people stood on the matter of death.

When my father died, my world was turned upside down, an upheaval that surprised me in its abysmal depth. I was advised, many times, to "move on," because that's what "he would want," that "time will heal." There were other clichés, but these are the most prominent ones that I can recall.

But Hurwitz writes in her book that "Judaism says: No, actually, you are not okay. The secular world might expect us to act like nothing has happened, but Judaism certainly doesn't." That to me is relatable, a realistic way for me to interface with the death of someone so central to my life. I didn't want to move on, even if I could. I wanted to remember, to hold our relationship close, to feel it. To me, this is the opposite of "getting on" with one's life and instead a process that seems more human—and humane. When I die, I'm quite certain that I don't want my daughters to "move on," because at that point, my essence would cease to exist. Even the Kaddish, the Jewish death prayer, is simple: Praise God, have faith even when someone close to you dies.

This all made sense to me but what about the afterlife that I heard so much about in Catholicism?

Well, that too is different for Jews.

As best as I could discover, there is no quid pro quo in Jewish life. In other words, a certain (presumably, good) behavior does not result in an afterlife that serves as a reward for a lifetime of being a "good" person. In fact, there is very little mention of an afterlife in any of what I read about Judaism. Instead, the Jewish emphasis seems to be on right now, on this life, instead of something waiting for us (perhaps) when we die. The focus is on *this* world, not any other world. As Rabbi Abraham Joshua Heschel notes, "There is no craving for death in the history of Jewish piety. . . . Earthly life, mortal life, is precisely the arena where the covenant between God and man must be fulfilled. . . . Life here and now is the task."

This also made sense to me, especially if one has the philosophy, as I do, that time is a precious commodity—there isn't enough of it, a way of thinking that I continually had reinforced while working in the hospital with terminally ill patients. They taught me about time, about living life for now. It was the most precious gift I have ever received, the one I cherish every day. I try to live my life forever cognizant of these teachings.

Hurwitz writes this about the Jewish people: "I used to wonder why, when people were so often trying to kill us, we didn't seek to comfort ourselves by making the afterlife our primary focus. In some ways, that might have been the more humane thing to do. But we never made that choice. Maybe that's one of the reasons why we're still here—because we refused to give up on this world or devalue this life, even if we didn't always get as much of it as we would have liked."

For a people that have often faced death, or even outright elimination, whether during the Holocaust, on October 7, or the countless other times, "Judaism tells us: To choose life so that we may live."

I can live with that. Pun intended.

CHAPTER FIVE

THE MESSAGE

New Orleans, September 2024

Baldwin & Co. bookstore, New Orleans

Baldwin & Co. is a Black-owned independent bookstore in the Gentilly section of New Orleans that proudly states on its website that it promotes "using the power of books to inspire social justice" and a "vibrant community hub, and a center for intellectual discovery where authors, readers, artists and activists gather in a welcoming and supportive environment." The store primarily carries titles by people of color, particularly those who write about the most relevant issues of the day. I have frequented Baldwin many times, sometimes alone and sometimes with my mother. It has a coffee shop in it, a quiet place to read, write, and sip a café au lait.

The owner of the bookstore is a man named DJ Johnson who I hadn't met until a mutual friend introduced me to him via text message. Soon after, DJ and I scheduled a call to talk about an upcoming event at Baldwin.

From the onset of the video call, I found DJ bright, engaging and quite committed to a cause that he—and I—cared deeply about: literacy among the underserved community in New Orleans. He told me about the work that Baldwin and Co. was doing in this area, and I relayed to him that I would be willing to get involved.

"How can I help?" I asked.

"There is one thing coming up that you could help us with," he told me. "Baldwin is sponsoring a book event with Ta-Nehisi Coates. Have you heard about his new book *The Message*?"

Oh yeah, I thought to myself, *I sure have.*

Coates's book had received widespread notoriety—press reports that had gone viral, due primarily to how he portrayed the Israeli-Palestinian conflict, its origins and its current status. According to the reviews that I read about *The Message*, depending on the source, Coates either presented a clear-eyed view of how Israel has handled the Palestinian situation, portraying the Jewish nation an "apartheid state," or Coates was a blatant anti-Semite who had a limited understanding of the complexities of the conflict and whose analysis was poorly considered. And that might be understating the venom expressed by those that held this view. The assessment of his work ran the gamut in the press I consumed—and seemed to depend entirely on one's own biases about the historical and current situation in that part of the world.

I didn't share any of what I had heard about the book with DJ, what I had read and how I interpreted it. I was sure DJ had read the same articles and even more sure that he had his own opinion about Coates's book and perhaps about that part of the world. But since I was being asked to help sponsor the event, to attach my name and that of my consulting firm to it if I did so, I felt that I would be tacitly endorsing the arguments put forth by Coates in his book. I quickly decided that to be fair, I needed to read *The Message* myself and not simply rely on someone else's interpretation of it.

"Thanks, DJ, for the information—and for what you do for our city. Let me think about it. I'll be back in touch."

I hung up the call and downloaded the book on my e-reader.

Following the path of the slave trade, the first parts of the book center on the visits Coates made to Senegal and South Carolina. In the last third of the book, Coates writes about his ten-day visit to Israel and Palestine, commenting mostly on the Israeli occupation and specifically the treatment of the Palestinians that he sees as unjust and immoral. In fact, he finds similarities in the way the Israelis handle the Palestinian population with the way Whites oppressed Black people using Jim Crow laws and the "separate but equal" doctrine. Whether it's Israeli soldiers blocking entrance into the Aqsa Mosque or the Israeli government cutting off the water supply into Gaza, Coates misses no opportunity to demonize the actions of the Israelis without putting the origins of the conflict into any sort of context. Perhaps in the most glaring example of the one-sidedness of his discussion, Coates doesn't even mention the October 7 attack by Hamas on innocent Israeli citizens—not once.

I finished the book in two sittings. Coates's writing is clear and personal, expressing well the raw emotion he felt when considering these topics. Unfortunately, his arguments about the Israeli-Palestinian conflict lacked depth, his understanding of the situation seemingly not informed by any more than his observations during a relatively brief visit to the area. In that way, the book disappointed—it didn't add light to this complex problem and, in fact, did something much worse. Coates made it seem that this was a simple example of an over-armed aggressor oppressing a blameless victim. There is much more to this story than that—and I have a feeling that Coates knows this to be true. He is too intelligent not to. But the way he presented his interpretation of the issue speaks for itself.

I finished the book, and after taking a day or two to process Coates's thesis, I emailed DJ and let him know that I would not be sponsoring the book event—and I told him why: Coates's book did not merely present a side of the story with which I disagreed, but rather it was a sloppy oversimplification of an immensely complicated issue. DJ of course understood and was quite gracious in his gratitude for my considering his request.

As I finished checking my email inbox, my mind couldn't help but drift toward a topic that I did have some concern about: the literacy program that Baldwin & Co. organized. One of the most prominent first books for this initiative would be *The Message.* Hundreds of young people would get a free copy at the upcoming event and, presumably, the book would be one of their first contacts with the conflict—or more precisely, the characterization of the conflict by Ta-Nehisi Coates. I closed my laptop and took a deep breath. That notion made me sad.

* * *

In the span of less than a few months, I had engaged in a heated discussion with a protester who was half my age and declined an invitation to be a sponsor of a book event that purportedly would benefit under-resourced children who desperately needed a book in their hands.

What was going on?

A Catholic by official identification, I now identified more with the many Jews across the world who were fighting for their religion, for their way of life, and even for their right to exist. I was now, for the first time, fighting with them, acting like their ally, because I *was* their ally. I took up the fight, yes, for them and for me, but also for the people that I have described in this book, the people who came before me, the ones I call my family.

In his book, Coates included a quote from an early Zionist named Moses Hess that was increasingly resonating with me. Regarding the efforts of German Jews to integrate, Hess said the following: "You may mask yourself a thousand times over; you may change your name, religion, and character; you may travel through the world incognito, so that people may not recognize the Jew in you; yet every insult to the Jewish name will strike you even more than the honest man who admits his Jewish loyalties and who fights for the honor of the Jewish name."

I've reread this quote dozens of times. It could have been written especially for me.

I was defending the Jewish people not because they couldn't defend themselves but because I had learned through my own family's experience what happens when you don't do that. You end up ostracized—some sent on a boat to another country, others on a train to a death camp. I wouldn't "travel through the world incognito" any longer, not while I had a choice, not after what I had learned.

I had gotten *The Message* but perhaps not the one Mr. Coates intended to deliver.

Instead, it was time for me to pick a side.

But first, there was a trip I needed to make, a place that I had to go and then call it quits, my exploration complete, my soul rested, my faith finally a settled matter.

CHAPTER SIX

KIPPENHEIM AND BUCHENWALD

March 2025

The Schmieheim Cemetery, South Baden, 2025

THE ZURICH AIRPORT WAS JUST WAKING UP WHEN I LANDED there on an early March morning in 2025.

Bleary-eyed from the long flight, I met a German guide named Rainer who I would later learn was a former engineer at Porsche. Driving north to Kippenheim, we talked about politics in our two countries, German cars, sports—and a bit about why I wanted to visit the area. I told him the reason was simple: I had to go. I wanted to see it, to feel it, to walk the streets my ancestors did. I didn't want to see pictures any more, I didn't want to read another book about it. I wanted to see it with my own eyes. To be clear, I didn't expect to run into any leftover Weills. They were gone, dead of natural or unnatural causes. But I could imagine how they lived, even see where they lived—and were laid to rest.

The roads along the way were lined with barren trees amid pastures that seemed to go on forever. A handful of scattered vineyards made me think of the few times that I had drunk German wine with a Swiss neighbor long ago. Travel fatigue getting the best of me, I soon closed my eyes against the late winter sun, trying as best I could to shake off the effects of the long flight while at the same time wondering what awaited me up the road.

There was a robust Jewish community in Kippenheim until the Holocaust. What about now? What artifacts remained of a community that no longer existed? Deep inside of me, I wanted to see what was there, what was left. Prior to leaving the States, I decided to visit two important historical sites: the Jewish cemetery in a small village near Kippenheim called Schmieheim, and the former synagogue in Kippenheim, now a memorial that commemorates the history of the Jewish community there.

Our first stop was the synagogue where I meet Jurgen Stude. Jurgen heads a local organization that fights anti-Semitism, and I arranged to meet him a few weeks before my arrival.

When we met, I could tell right away that Jurgen was a serious person, probably in his seventies, a man of few words—except when it came to the Jewish experience in Kippenheim. Through my travel fog, I tried to absorb everything he said, hoping to grasp the texture as a way to supplement all that I read about the place.

"Let's take a walk first," Jurgen said. There was hardly a person in sight as we made our way down narrow cobblestone streets. Just a block from the synagogue, we stopped in front of a building that had the word “Metzger” on the front. “What does that mean?” I asked.

“Butcher.” Jurgen said, simulating cutting meat, a game of pantomime between someone who spoke no German and another who only spoke a little English. As we stood in front and I took in the earth-colored façade, Jurgen asked, “Do you know who lived here?”

“A butcher?” I guessed, not unreasonably given what I had just learned. Jurgen laughed and said, “No. One of your family members.”

“Oh yeah? Which one?”

“Albert Weill.” The composer Kurt’s father.

I had another look. The shop wasn’t open yet so we couldn’t go in. But what would I see anyway in the converted building? I just stood there for a few moments, had a look down the street. This was enough. It just felt good to be in the same spot as one of my ancestors. It felt really good, it felt right.

On the way back to the synagogue, Jurgen had one other thing to show me. “Do you know what a Stolperstein is?” he asked.

Yes, I did.

I recalled the one morning in Berlin a couple years prior when, desperately looking for my father’s boyhood home, I came upon dozens of tiny gold plaques embedded in the stone sidewalks in the neighborhood where my father’s family had lived. I even remembered the names of those who had been hauled out of their homes, loaded on trucks and trains, headed to the camps, to squalid living conditions and fear, and, eventually, worse.

“Yeah. I know what Stolpersteins are.”

Jurgen nodded. “Come with me.”

We walked a few more blocks and stopped in front of a nondescript home that looked a bit like a gingerbread house, a brown front with small windows and wooden beams facing a busy street. We stood and looked at the house for a few minutes. I waited for Jurgen to tell me the significance of what I was looking at, but he remained silent. I turned to look at him, hoping he would get to the punch line.

He looked down, staring, it seemed, at my feet. I, in turn, looked down and saw what he wanted to show me: two Stolpersteins, the morning sun reflecting back up at me off the shiny golden plaques. I got down on one knee to have a closer look.

Claire Weill

Hans Leopold Weill

"Do you know these two?"

I struggled to recall who they were, only vaguely remembering their names from the family genealogy that I referenced often while working on this project.

"Uh, yeah, I've seen their names before."

"Claire was the mother. Hans Weill was the son. He immigrated to the UK in 1938, then Australia ultimately." Hans was, of course, also my father's name, so seeing his name on the plaque was a bit disconcerting.

Even though I had obviously never met this person, one of my relatives, I was relieved that he got out, making it to freedom and away from the Nazis.

"What about Claire?" I asked.

Jurgen shook his head. "She died."

"In one of the camps?" I asked, shielding my eyes, looking up from my kneeling position.

"No. By suicide. She knew what was coming. She arranged for her son to leave . . . then killed herself."

"Oh," I said. I looked back down at the plaque. What a wrenching decision so many had to make during this period.

What would I have done? I asked myself for the thousandth time since I began the research for this book.

I stood back up. It was time to have a look at the synagogue.

Built in 1850, the Kippenheim synagogue served the local congregation until its desecration in November 1938. Thereafter, the building was primarily used for storage. From 1986 to 1989 its exterior was restored to its original conditions with the financial support of Israeli industrialist Stef Wertheimer who left Kippenheim with his family in 1937. The cost of restoring the synagogue was estimated at around 2.5 million German marks, which is more than a million US dollars.

Jurgen and I walked inside the iron gate of the synagogue. In the outer foyer, a small written memorial hung on the wall, listing all of the names of the Kippenheim Jews who perished in the Holocaust. I quickly scanned the list and found five relatives of mine: Berta, Gerda, Helene, Julius, and another, different Claire. I knew about them, had seen their names in various documents and books that I had read. But there was something about seeing their names written, among all the others, in this sacred place, in this town that was such an integral part of our family's legacy. I read the list of names several times, to take in each individually, to give them their due.

I paused for a moment before I went inside, with Jurgen standing nearby, kindly giving me the luxury of time.

The synagogue was surprisingly small, no bigger than a children's classroom, but the high soaring ceilings gave the place an airy feel nonetheless. On one of the walls was a timeline that carefully documented the history of the synagogue, its place in the Jewish fabric of the town, its desecration when the Nazis came to power, and its use today as a place where lectures took place about the anti-Semitism that was rapidly spreading throughout the world. I studied the walls closely and ran my hands over the jagged cracks, feeling their texture, white chalky dust covering my palms and fingertips. I didn't wipe off the remnants of that wall for the rest of the day.

My next stop was the Jewish cemetery southwest of Kippenheim in a small village called Schmieheim, which was established in the seventeenth century. Until the nineteenth century, Schmieheim had more than five hundred Jewish inhabitants and a rabbi. The graveyard also served Jewish communities in Altdorf, Ettenheim, Friesenheim, Lahr, Nonnweiler, Orschweier, and Rut. Extensively damaged in 1938, the cemetery was restored by remedial work after the war. Despite this, relics from centuries past can still be found in the graveyard. Long after the Holocaust, inspired by the stories of survivors in the area, the mayor of Kippenheim, Willi Mathis, commissioned a two-volume book that listed the names of every person buried in the cemetery.

The area had lush green trees surrounding pastures that spread out over rolling hills. On a gentle slope near a two-way road, the cemetery stretched to the top of the hill. At the bottom of the hill were rows and rows of crumbling tombstones, adorned with names written in Hebrew. Some of the names could be easily discerned, but many had become unreadable due to weather exposure and vegetation overgrowth. As I walked up the hill, placing my hand on decaying tombstones along the way, I noticed that some of the gravesites were in much better shape than others, obviously having undergone restoration. I spent thirty minutes going row by row, reading the names, kneeling at times to get a closer look. One thing became clear: Many of the people buried there had the same last name as me.

Moses Weil
Charlotte Weil
Jsak Weil
Leopold Weil
Nathan Weil
Helene Weill

There were others.

I made it to the top of the hill and spent several minutes surveying the cemetery from this high vantage point. I turned up the collar on my jacket as a strong cold breeze blew in dark, gray clouds. Taking in the magnitude of the place, my eyes traced rows and rows of gravesites that seemed to go on forever, blanketing the hillside. In all, five thousand souls had been laid to rest in the ground beneath me.

I thought for a few moments about how I came to this place, why I had come all this way, why it was important to me to actually see it, a place I hadn't even heard of just a handful of months ago.

But I did know why—it felt like one of the final pieces in the puzzle, an experience that few people get to have, to visit an area that was populated with one's own people going back hundreds of years. I thought just then about what burial ceremonies must have been like centuries ago, when extended Weill family members would gather at gravesites to put to rest one of their own. Tears were likely shed, hugs exchanged, no different from how it is now. I couldn't help but think of my own burial, a morbid thought but one I couldn't avoid standing there that day. I wouldn't be around to see it, of course, but I did think about how few of my family members would witness it—our family has been drastically reduced, culled down by horrific circumstances.

And then a disheartening thought: Our clan wouldn't only be reduced. It would soon be extinguished. There were so few of us left, that was true, an undeniable fact that had been put into stark context by visiting the place where my family had originated. That was what this trip was about. Context. I had that now, and for that I am profoundly grateful to have embarked on this journey so many months ago.

My trip to Kippenheim was done. There wasn't much else to see. I had visited the few remnants left of my family's history in this tiny village tucked away in southwest Germany. All that I could do now was turn to more recent history, to a period a bit more than eighty years ago, when the Nazis plan for the Jewish people came into clear focus.

All that was left, at least for me, at this time, was Buchenwald.

"Why is it way the hell out here?" I asked Rainer, my impatience with time spent on the road getting the best of me. It was a rhetorical question I realized as soon as the words left my mouth. "You think they were trying to hide what they were doing, or what?" Rainer smiled at me grimly in the rearview mirror. "I suspect so," he said.

It was time for a visit to a place that I didn't really want to go. But I had to go—after October 7 and its aftermath, after all this searching, after the journey I had embarked on. It was time to go, to face it. The journey had chosen me, and it was now telling me to go to Buchenwald.

Much could be discovered without actually taking the trouble to see it firsthand. There are books and pictures, firsthand accounts and testimonials. But because of the role Buchenwald played in my family's destiny, it would no longer do to keep the place at arm's distance. It was time to see it, to feel it.

The road to the camp twisted and turned through open fields with large windmills, then along narrow stone streets through towns that seemed to be only a few blocks long. We passed backyards with laundry hanging on the lines and an old couple walking on the sidewalk holding hands. Schoolchildren carried brightly colored backpacks that reminded me of my own kids when they were little.

What must it be like to live out here? I thought, in not only a remote area but in the shadow of one of the most notorious Nazi concentration camps. We crossed paths with huge buses, presumably filled with people like me who wanted to have a look at the place. Rainer would pull over to one side of the street, perilously close to the sidewalk, to let the buses pass, giving the drivers a quick wave as they motored by.

Finally the road opened up, and we were there.

At first blush, the sight wasn't very impressive. A row of old brown barracks stood next to an ample parking area, one large enough to accommodate both cars and buses. I came to find out that the barracks that once housed Nazi soldiers was now used as dormitory space for young people who came to visit the camp—a retreat of sorts, to learn about what happened there.

We got out of the van and stretched our legs after the long drive. "Well," I said, arching my back. "Let's take a walk, shall we."

"Lead the way," Rainer replied.

Before my trip to Germany, I had read a great deal about Buchenwald—the camp layout, what went on there, how many prisoners perished—so I knew where I wanted to go first: the stone quarry.

During my grandfather's time at the camp, he drew the unenviable assignment of working in the quarry, forced to carry massive rocks from one side of the camp to the other and back again, all day long for seven weeks, with no particular purpose other than to abuse the prisoners—and if some died while doing their work, so be it. Now, seven weeks in most of our lives is a blink, passing with lightning speed. But standing at the top of a bluff overlooking the former quarry, I thought that, for my grandfather, those seven weeks must have seemed like an eternity.

From the high vantage point, I could see the entire space, now less of a quarry than a quarter-mile-long crater covered with broken-up stones sitting in green and brown grassy areas. I imagined Nazi soldiers watching over the prisoners in the very spot where I now stood, perhaps having a cigarette and casual conversation with their colleagues, and maybe sharing a laugh when one of the prisoners fell from exhaustion. I pictured my grandfather hauling the stones, a small man, breathing in dust that would eventually sicken him, his prison uniform in taters, his skin falling off his bones, his eyes sunken. I turned to look for where the electrical fence might have been, the one that prisoners assigned to this area would purposely run into to end their life under their own terms rather than endure this unimaginable suffering.

I walked down a narrow road that led to the quarry bottom and spent time roaming the area, not sure exactly what I was looking for. Rainer was a hundred meters away, doing the same thing, wandering.

After thirty minutes or so, satisfied that I had seen it, I started to walk toward the road that would take me to the rest of the camp. But before I did, I bent down and picked up a rock the size of a baseball. I tossed it into the air a few times and put it in my coat pocket. This one was coming home with me. I'd put it next to my other rocks: the one from Kilimanjaro that I picked up during my climb in 2002, the one from Mount Ventoux in France that I collected from the side of the road when I cycled up it in 2005, and the oldest one in my "collection," the piece from the Berlin Wall that I had knocked off with my umbrella tip during a visit there in 1990, just a few months after the Wall fell.

I wondered just then if I was desecrating sacred ground by taking a piece of it back home with me, but then decided that it was probably okay. My grandfather wouldn't mind—and in that moment, his was the only opinion that mattered to me.

I started back up the hill, feeling the weight of that rock in my pocket—and glad, again, that I had made the trip.

When Rainer dropped me off at the Frankfurt airport, my journey complete, we shook hands at the curb after I collected my luggage. The parting was bittersweet in a surprising way. I had only just met this man, but he was about my age, had two kids about my daughters' age, and we had spent a significant amount of time driving through the German countryside, chatting about a wide range of topics.

"Send me the book when it's done," he said.

"Will do," I said. "Tell me what you think of it." Then I smiled. "And if you don't like it, *don't* leave a review on Amazon."

"I'll like it, I'm sure."

We stood for a few moments in awkward silence. "Are you glad you came?" he asked. I think he knew the answer to that one.

"I am."

"You know, it occurred to me while we were driving around, that your main interests in life have been in two areas: Saving lives on the one hand, and now this, studying the destruction of life on the other hand." He tilted his head to one side. "Have you ever thought about that?"

I looked away for a second, thinking, and then back to him. "No, I haven't. Not until this moment."

He leaned in, embracing me. "Safe travels, my friend."

I shouldered my backpack and rolled my suitcase into the terminal. It was time to travel.

CHAPTER SEVEN

MY (SECOND) AWAKENING—TOWARD COMPLETION

Alys Beach, Florida, April 2025

Sabbath, New Orleans, 2025

In the Author's Note of this book, I wrote that tribalism is a dominant part of the human experience, the want—really, the innate need—to identify as one thing or the other. Throughout the journey of completing this work, I have become convinced that the best way to feel complete, perhaps the *only* way to feel complete, is to come to terms with who we are and where we came from—to gain a clear-eyed understanding without the ambiguity and self-deception that can make how one identifies simply a matter of strategic calculation or positioning.

So after all this, what's my story? What did I find out about David Weill—and, by extension, the people around me and those who have similar struggles?

I realize this now: My parents changed the course of both of their family histories, my mother by choice, my father by force. There is the A-roll of my life—my immediate family seen from my current vantage point—the main storyline of my own experience. This is coupled with an accessory B-roll: the journey of my ancestors that I didn't know much about—until now. Both are significant. There is not one without the other.

The strength of my lineage is hard to ignore—and given that deep heritage, it defies reason that it didn't heavily shape who I became. The Weill family was a prominent Jewish one who for centuries were leaders in their community—a heritage that was shattered by the Nazis. Had the Nazis not come to power and paved a path of death and destruction, then presumably the Weill family would have continued on in Germany and would have marked its seven hundredth year of its known existence in 2020. It is also clear to me that my grandfather was the inflection point, the secular one who bore the brunt of my immediate family's experience with the Holocaust. He also ushered in the American Weills who, given the dynamics present in those of us who are his descendants, will extinguish relatively soon. There aren't many of us left.

If my grandfather was the inflection point of our family, as I believe he was, it is also clear to me that since he could not have made it to America without the more famous Kurt Weill, the composer deserves a great deal of credit for the family continuing in any form—and for my being here to write these words.

My grandfather, and therefore my father, were destitute and in tatters when they came to this country, and both bore the burden of that experience as long as they lived. I bore some of it as well because I was raised by a man who had gone through significant trauma. My children have not, and hopefully never will, experience anything of this kind. My family is stable and secure in every way that stability and security can be measured. My children have no safety concerns, no financial burdens, two loving parents, and first-class educational opportunities to fall back on—and they have no issue with religious identity. My daughters are Catholic and, as far as I can tell, have never given their Catholicism, or its relevance to them, a second thought. All of this helps me sleep at night. That is their inheritance. I am proud to have helped provide it, but I know there was luck and circumstance involved that I had nothing to do with.

My father, through no fault of his own, didn't process his emotions about his trauma, so it never resolved. His generation handled their emotions differently than mine. Theirs was not the therapy generation, the one of self-help books, antidepressants, and Dr. Phil. My generation, and especially my children's, is one of sharing, of feelings being validated. I learned all those qualities late in life, after crisis hit and I began to question everything about me, about my role in the universe—a phrase that seems self-involved but is an accurate way to describe my situation. My father let his emotions sit and fester inside of him and passed that inheritance to me and my sisters. It wasn't his fault. In many ways, I have sympathy for my father, although on the surface he was not someone who evoked this kind of emotion, given that he was a successful and highly intelligent man, sure of himself, at least outwardly. But he had something inside of him that he never addressed, and I am not sure he ever tried. I don't think he knew how to.

I had it easy, he would say at times. But he didn't have to say it. I knew it; it was obvious. My life was cushy and, therefore, his main parenting philosophy seemed to be: *You better succeed, you're expected to succeed.* Mine is a life that has epitomized starting out on third base, as the saying goes, so I was made to feel that the only one that could make my life hard was me. At times, this searching, sometimes tortured, brain of mine has done just that.

Like many authors before me, I have used writing as a path toward understanding. My first book, *Exhale,* dug into my professional life, my relationship to being a transplant doctor, the lives lost and saved, the rollercoaster that I rode every day until I could no longer do it, culminating in a messy dismount, dizzying in its suddenness and personal devastation. My second book, a novel called *All That Really Matters,* was set around a transplant surgeon with issues. My protagonist's experiences were not identical to mine but close enough that in nearly every promotional interview that I gave, the question was asked, *Is the story in the book your story? Is Dr. Joe Bosco you?*

No, I said. I brushed off the question, deftly redirecting inquiries of this sort to safer grounds. But yes, the story was partly mine, reimagined in a way that revealed what would have happened if my own life had taken a left turn instead of a right, if I had made different choices, come to different decisions, chosen other paths. In both books, I was working out my "stuff" on the page. In casual conversation, perhaps over drinks and dinner, I have often used a different "S" word.

People that read the books knew that—and told me as much. It was on the page for all to see, in the most unambiguous language that I could muster.

And now comes this work, digging into the "why" of all that my previous life was. Herein, I have explained the basis for what I did, how I was wired for it, how much of what was going to happen in my life was predetermined even before I was born. That is the real inheritance we all have from those who came before us, not the kind of inheritance that is written into a will somewhere, pulled out of a dusty drawer in an attorney's office when a relative dies. No, this is the *real* inheritance. And like everyone else, I take the good from those that came before me and the bad. I pray that I can learn to fully accept both.

When sitting down for the first time to write my next book, I am like most authors in that I have little idea what direction the new work will take. My basic idea for this project was to explore religious identity, using my ancestry and own experiences as a vague outline and based on the feeling that without a religion to call one's own, one can feel like a gypsy, moving from town to town without a real anchor.

But the book didn't turn out to be just about *religious* identity—it's about identity, period, which may make the subject matter more expansive but at the same time, opaque. That was not purposeful. This identity thing is hard to wrestle to the ground, which may have come through in these pages.

The search has led me to Berlin, the Black church in New Orleans, the Edmund Pettis Bridge and the synagogue in Selma, the Palo Alto Catholic Church where I was baptized and pulled from the abyss—a deep descent that was equal parts fate and destiny. It took me to New York, Israel, and Miami. But the journey revealed here changed the way I think about myself, my own identity, and of course, about religious affiliation. I was no longer vaguely connected to Judaism or the Jewish people, I was just connected.

As much confusion as I've had on the question of religious identity, I believe now that the uncertainty went even further than one of whether I should go to synagogue on Saturdays or church on Sundays. The dilemma instead was about the core of who I was when I woke up in the morning. For most of my life the easy way out was an emotionally detached but outwardly noble one: I was a transplant doctor. My role in life was to save lives. Full stop. No more, no less. That was the costume I spent all of my adult life wearing. But as that time in the hospital fades away in my rearview mirror—distant memories I cherish but that have started to recede—I am left with the question: *Now what?*

It has grown clearer for me, as I sit in my home office and write, dogs at my feet, a candle glowing, hot tea within easy reach. I glance at what I have chosen to occupy my writing space, the most cherished real estate of any writer, the place that is most revealing about her. A cross hangs from my desk lamp, right above a silver Star of David that I recently bought. Against the wall sits a bookshelf, a prominent section of which is a literal *Who's Who* of authors who have written about the rise of Nazi Germany and the Holocaust: Primo Levi, Hannah Arendt, Elie Wiesel, Robert Jay Lifton, William Shirer, just to name a few. A photograph of our maid Deborah and me at my mother's eightieth birthday party. A Catholic Bible sits on another shelf, as do a few books by Richard Rohr. There's a painting of Muhammad Ali in white boxing trunks and red gloves, looking straight at me, someone else who belonged and didn't belong—and found their true religion later in life—and a black-and-white photograph of a young Kurt Weill, my grandfather, his arm around Kurt Weill, the composer, in Bavaria, broad smiles on their face, the happiness of youth, before the rest happened.

The tapestry of my spiritual life, all in one place, so close I could touch it whenever I felt the need.

We are all a patchwork of disparate parts, some more than others. Maybe I am more than most—a descendent of generations of rabbis, a German Jew father, a Southern Baptist mother, one grandfather in a concentration camp, another likely in the Klan, with a Black churchgoer as my second mother. I married a devout Catholic and eventually became one when I reached age fifty. At times, some of these people played more important roles than others but none ever left me, or were fully embraced, no matter how hard I tried. I walked around every day of my now sixty years with all these people inside me, parts that were at times discrete, at other times, not, but often in conflict, a confusing legacy that I kept in a closet, because it was the easier—not better—path.

The last time I found a religion, my wife and daughters' Catholicism, there was a structured process involved: the RCIA classes, the baptism in front of family and friends, the cross around my neck. I thought then, foolishly it turns out, that this would settle the matter once and for all.

It didn't, as must now be obvious.

This time, the discovery happened in the quiet of my mind, by the reading and contemplation in the solitary confines of my home office, in hotel rooms, on plane flights. This time, I was circling back home after a journey of the mind and heart, a clear-eyed look at where I came from in the seventh decade of my life. Better late than never, one could say. This time, the transformation played out over a few years, discreet episodes that I've described in these pages.

This journey was not something I planned out, plotting years in advance to scramble my religious identity so I could find a new one. *Maybe Episcopalian this time? Or Muslim? I've heard Buddhism is cool.* No, it didn't happen this way. This story announced itself, it chased me when I didn't necessarily want to be chased. But isn't that the way it is with all that haunts us, with everything in our lives that is unresolved? We can't hide, not if we want a chance at contentment. The body knows and the mind knows. Neither can be fooled, as hard as we often try.

But "owning" my Judaism isn't only about accepting one's religion into one's life. It's more than that—it's accepting my family, my ancestors, for who they are, what they stood for, and what they endured. Their struggle made my life possible, the privilege to wander here and there with my own thoughts and ambitions, the peace I was gifted to study and consider my own plight. I had these luxuries. They were given to me, the most precious gift in a life that has been charmed in so many ways. I didn't have to fight, flee, or die to have any of it. All I had to do was walk a path to find what was missing from my life, an examination that was not met with violence or any kind of existential threat. It was mine for the taking and I could do it my way, which I dare say was a rabbinical way, by quiet contemplation and deep discussions about what I was discovering, what I was learning. In the most important ways, I had done it like my ancestors had, all the generations going back to Juda Weill, born in the fourteenth century.

But there was one important question that I still needed to address—and a nagging one at that: *What do I feel about Catholicism now?*

Love, unending gratitude, for doing nothing less than saving me when I needed it the most.

Catholicism is like an ex-lover now for whom I only hold the utmost respect and fond memories of the times we had. I am in awe of Catholicism and all it espouses, all it stands for, the good it has provided in this world—which, I might add, far outweighs any of the bad that receives so much attention. I am not turning away from Catholicism so much as I am embracing Judaism, because it is mine, always was. It just took me a while to get there.

Or as the Yiddish poet Jacob Glatstein put it: "Inside me sits the soul of an ancestor who summons me back." Yes, Mr. Glatstein, that is what has happened to me. Judaism has called me back. It let me be confused, it allowed me to wander, and it has waited on me. As the title of Sarah Hurwitz's impactful book suggests, Judaism was *Here All Along.*

I'm glad it was.

For when describing her relationship with Judaism, Blu Greenberg once wrote, "It has chosen me and I have chosen it back."

Yes. That's exactly right. This time, I know so.

Rosh Hashanah Service, Watersound, Florida, 2024

EPILOGUE

ROSH HASHANAH AT SEA SHUL

Along County Road 30a, Florida

A COUPLE THAT WE KNEW FROM MEMPHIS ASKED JACKIE and me to a Rosh Hashanah service. As with most things we did socially, Jackie got the details and relayed them to me.

"A Rosh Hashanah service? In Florida? Is there a synagogue down there?" I asked.

Jackie shrugged her shoulders. "I don't know. I can read you the text." She pulled up the messages on her phone. "It says the service is at the Watersound Beach Club." Watersound was a coastal community, one of dozens, set along a small two way county road called 30a that ran along the Gulf front. "There's dinner—and I guess a service of some sort."

"I wonder what the service will be like?" I asked, more rhetorically than anything else.

Jackie smiled. "You're asking me?"

"Well, I don't know either. You know my story, right?"

"Sure do," she said. "Let's go, though. See what it's all about. Could be interesting"

I gave it a few moments thought. "Okay . . . I guess so. Tell them we'll be there."

The event was held in an outdoor patio and grill area near a massive swimming pool. The Gulf of Mexico was off in the distance, the smell of salt water filled the thick air with each wind gust. A volunteer greeted us at a table that was set up by the pool. She was in her forties, friendly, and asked if I was a member of the Sea Shul.

"The what?" I asked.

"The Sea Shul," she said again, perhaps thinking I didn't hear her the first time.

"Umm, no . . . I don't think so."

She laughed. "Well you would know if you were."

Maybe, I thought, *maybe*.

She asked us our names, wrote them each on a paper name tag, and handed them to us.

"What is a shul?" Jackie asked as we walked toward the gathered crowd.

"I don't know," I said. I got my phone out and opened up the browser. I put on my reading glasses. "It says a shul is a school or synagogue." We both took a look around. There was an outdoor bar, a pool with lounge chairs, TVs hanging in each corner, just barely far enough away from the rotating ceiling fans.

Didn't look like a school or a synagogue, not that I would know much about what the latter looked like.

"I guess this is kind of a beach synagogue," I said. Just then, I thought, *I have a lot to learn*, but not in an overwhelming or depressing way—in a curious one.

We walked to the bar. *Why not get a glass of wine?* Just to fit in with the others who were doing the same. As we waited on our wine, I turned to Jackie and said, "Just like Catholic church, huh?" The bartender appeared with two glasses of wine, one red, one white. "Yeah. Exactly. Just like it," she said and clinked my glass.

We sat at a dinner table set for eight. The other couples at the table were about our age and attired in typical evening beach wear, loose-fitting linen shorts and cotton shirts for the men, sundresses for the women, sandals. All were tan and fit. All seemed delightful.

After a few introductions and small talk, the woman sitting next to me asked where I attended synagogue. *Here we go.* I caught Jackie out of the corner of my eye, smiling then looking away.

"My synagogue?" I asked. "Well . . . here, I guess," I said and gestured casually at the other tables nearby.

The woman frowned. "No, I mean regularly."

I started speaking in shorthand. "Not affiliated with any synagogue. Taking a little break right now." I could feel Jackie kick me under the table. And with that, the questions stopped for the night. I was really looking forward to having a better answer for that question soon, but I didn't have it just yet.

The night went on. Songs were sung, with a few prayers interspersed by a rabbi from Atlanta who came in for the service. There were smiles all around, hugs, and hand holding. Little children ran around with unbridled glee. It was beautiful chaos. I looked over at Jackie who was taking it all in, a cradle Catholic at a religious service that looked nothing like the ones with which she was familiar. The whole scene made me smile. The food, the language, the customs were all foreign to me, but just then I thought back to the Baptist church of my youth, the one our maid, Deborah, would bring me to. On this night, there was singing and laughter, all just a year removed from the October 7 atrocities and the ongoing hostage crisis. I wasn't a 10/08 Jew, although the thought crossed my mind as I sat there. I was a 1360 Jew, the year my family's progenitor, Juda Weill, was born.

But that night by the beach, there was rapture, just as there was back then in that church in inner-city New Orleans, even when the rest of those folks' lives wasn't so easy. I closed my eyes. This was religion. This was it. Providing joy where there wasn't any, to me, to those who came before me, back in Germany, back in Selma.

After a half an hour or so, we all got up and walked to the beach—more prayers, more hugs, more chaos, more smiles from me and the others there. I suppose the night would have gone differently if we had attended services in a proper synagogue, but there we were, happily tucked away in our beach getaway, glad to have found another part of this Gulf community that we knew nothing about.

The next day when I was walking on the beach, I ran into one of the few Jews I knew in our particular beach town, who asked me what I did the previous night.

"You know, went to services." I said, smoothing out the powder-white sand with my bare feet.

"Rosh Hashanah services?" she asked, suppressing a laugh, it seemed. She knew about my angst regarding religion.

"Yeah. Services," I said, nodding in affirmation, like it was as natural for me as breathing in and out.

"You?" she asked.

I smiled and shrugged my shoulders.

Yeah, me, I thought. *Me.*

ACKNOWLEDGMENTS

I want to thank Writing. Many days, many hours, it was just the two of us—and you helped me more than you could know. I am reminded of a quote from the author Lidia Yuknavitch: "I am not alone. Whatever else there was or is, writing is with me." In my life, that's more true now than ever before.

Now, on to actual people. I'd like to thank my editor, Claire Wachtel, who believed in this project from the first time we talked about it—and well before I knew what I would find in my search and what was awaiting me at the end of the journey.

I would also like to thank the rest of the team at Union Square & Co., whose professionalism and commitment helped make this book the best it could be.

The premise for this book was first published as an essay for *Tablet Magazine*, and I am grateful to the editors for believing in this project when I was just starting to work through my own thoughts.

A special thanks to my agent, Marly Rusoff, who found a perfect home for this book—and who is truly a delightful person and someone with whom I feel privileged to work.

Doing introspective work like this requires time and space, and I appreciate the team at Weill Consulting Group for providing me with both, especially Pete Tafaro, my friend and colleague, who does a phenomenal job of smoothing my life's rough edges.

As always, there is no inspiration for me without music, and there is no music that inspires me to dig deep into my soul more than that produced by Terence Blanchard. You were with me every day when I sat down to write, even when you were off doing your thing elsewhere. Proud to know you, TB.

To my closest friends, as we get older, we need each other more than ever. We've discussed many topics in this book over the years (and a great deal more!), and you've helped me in ways that are hard to express. To each of you, I'm proud to be on your team.

To my sisters, Judy Weill and Leslie Ehret: Your job isn't easy. It's difficult to read about a life that you both shared, and while you may never have wanted a writer in your family, thanks for tolerating this one.

To Kurt Weill, my grandfather, who taught me what perseverance and determination look like under the most unimaginable circumstances. You're an inspiration.

To Kurt Weill, the composer, who I never met, but have learned from while doing the work for this project—especially how a creative life can be crafted to tell a story, make a statement, and communicate an idea. Oh, and you're probably the reason I am even here. So thanks for that.

To my mother, Kathy Weill, who inspired much of this book and, well, my life. Thanks, Mom. I hope we have many more books to discuss in the future, ones I've written and ones written by better authors.

To my father, Hans Weill, who was the bridge that connected me to the rich legacy of the Weill clan. I wish you were still around to read the words in this book, to see the light that was shone on the darkest corners of our family's past. But somehow, I think you know the story and what it has all meant to me.

To Hannah and Ava, you're everything in my world. My legacy is also yours and I'm humbled to be able to share it with you, but even more so to be your father, an identity that is my most cherished one—and one I've *never* struggled with. And to Jackie, who helped show me what faith can mean in one's life. For that, I'm grateful.

To the strangers I met along the way on this journey, especially the rabbis and the priests, in lands near and far. Our conversations made me realize that you understood what I was trying to do and when I faltered, you encouraged me to keep going. I needed that, more than once or twice.

Lastly, to my Hero and Protector. I needed someone to play both roles in my life, and there you were. You know what you mean to me.

ABOUT THE AUTHOR

Dr. David Weill is the former director of the Center for Advanced Lung Disease and Lung and Heart-Lung Transplant Program at Stanford University Medical Center. He is currently the principal of the Weill Consulting Group.

Dr. Weill's writing has appeared in the *Wall Street Journal, USA Today, Salon, Newsweek,* the *Chicago Tribune, STAT,* the *Washington Post, The Hill, LitHub, Tablet,* the *Times of Israel,* TODAY .com, and the *Los Angeles Times.* He also has been interviewed on Fox, CNN, and *The Doctors* television show, as well as by the *New York Times,* the *San Francisco Chronicle,* and the *Wall Street Journal.* Dr. Weill is the author of the memoir *Exhale: Hope, Healing, and a Life in Transplant* and the novel *All That Really Matters.*

For more information, please visit davidweill.com.

RAISING READERS

Books Build Bright Futures

Thank you for reading this book and for being a reader of books in general. As an author, I am so grateful to share being part of a community of readers with you, and I hope you will join me in passing our love of books on to the next generation of readers.

Did you know that reading for enjoyment is the single biggest predictor of a child's future happiness and success?

More than family circumstances, parents' educational background, or income, reading impacts a child's future academic performance, emotional well-being, communication skills, economic security, ambition, and happiness.

Studies show that kids reading for enjoyment in the US is in rapid decline:

- In 2012, 53% of 9-year-olds read almost every day. Just 10 years later, in 2022, the number had fallen to 39%.
- In 2012, 27% of 13-year-olds read for fun daily. By 2023, that number was just 14%.

Together, we can commit to **Raising Readers** and change this trend. How?

- Read to children in your life daily.
- Model reading as a fun activity.
- Reduce screen time.
- Start a family, school, or community book club.
- Visit bookstores and libraries regularly.
- Listen to audiobooks.
- Read the book before you see the movie.
- Encourage your child to read aloud to a pet or stuffed animal.
- Give books as gifts.
- Donate books to families and communities in need.

BOB1217

Books build bright futures, and **Raising Readers** is our shared responsibility.

For more information, visit **JoinRaisingReaders.com**

Sources: National Endowment for the Arts, National Assessment of Educational Progress, WorldBookDay.org, Nielsen BookData's 2023 "Understanding the Children's Book Consumer"